BREAK-

THROUGH

Creating a New Scorecard
for Group Ministry Success

BREAK-

THROUGH

KEN BRADDY

B&H
PUBLISHING
NASHVILLE, TENNESSEE

To Cindy Weatherall, my superfan in Pensacola, Florida. Your words of encouragement and your enthusiasm for the Bible teaching ministry of the church have been life-giving to me. Olive Baptist Church is blessed to have you on their staff. Thanks for being a fan and a friend.

Acknowledgments

To my wife, Tammy, who became a "book widow" as I wrote. Thank you for always supporting me as I serve the church and its leaders. And thanks for choosing the cover design!

I'm very grateful to Ron and Debbie Moore for allowing me to spend a few days in their wonderful cabin where I got this project launched. The quietness of your Eagles Rest retreat ministry gave me the environment in which I wrote multiple chapters of this book over a few short days, getting the work moving in the right direction, and enabling me to hit early deadlines. Thank you for continuing to serve the church through your Eagles Rest ministry.

I am thankful to the B&H team for shepherding this book. Taylor Combs, thanks for saying yes after meeting with your team! Logan Pyron and Kim Stanford, thank you for editing and sharpening my words and thoughts. Words create worlds, and I am thankful that together we created a world for group leaders and pastors to explore.

Finally, thanks to my long-time friend in ministry, Dr. Tod Tanner. Your feedback early on helped the book take shape. You spoke into it with a pastor's heart, especially a pastor who loves the Bible teaching ministry of the church and knows its importance in making disciples.

Contents

Measurement 3: Form Deeper Relationships

Measurement 4: Engage in Acts of Service

Preface

I love golf.

I was introduced to the game by A. J. (Joe) Downing, my grandfather or, as I called him, "Popsi." Later in life I learned that he was a Sunday School department director at University Baptist Church in Abilene, Texas. He was also a deacon. His ordination certificate and his Bible are in my home office.

In life he was right-handed, but in golf he was a leftie. He loved the game so much that he bought a used golf cart and hauled it to and from the golf course in the bed of his 1967 Chevy pickup truck. I remember he kept a pair of wood rails in the bed of that old truck, and it was terrifying to watch him load and unload that old golf cart, using the wood slats as makeshift ramps.

Popsi gave me my first set of golf clubs. When he and my grandmother came to visit, Popsi would always take me to the driving range at the University of Texas at Arlington. We'd hit buckets of practice balls for hours. I loved my time with him.

And then Popsi took me to play my first round of golf while my family was at his house for a visit. All I remember about my first round of golf was that he was patient and kind, and he had to keep telling me to pick up my ball so we could move on. I must have been holding up the pace of play. As time went on, I got better at golf. Better . . . not great. Golf is hard work! On the course I saw my first golf scorecard. Popsi kept score for both of us. The scorecard helped us keep track of who was winning. It was not even a contest in those early days!

The Golf Scorecard

Every course provides golfers with a scorecard and a small golf pencil at the beginning of their round. The scorecard measures two things: *the total number of shots made per hole and the total number of shots made per round.* That's it. The focus is on the total score. Nothing else is measured.

When golfing with a group of friends, scores matter. It is good etiquette for the person who just had the low score on a hole to tee off first on the next one. It is called "having honors."

The Old Scorecard for Groups

If you have been around group Bible studies for any amount of time, you have realized it also has a scorecard. Right or wrong, the old scorecard for groups has measured one thing: *the total number of people in Bible study each week.* That's not necessarily a bad measurement. We should be concerned about numbers. After all, numbers represent people.

"How many people were in your Bible study today?" is a question group leaders ask one another. We like to compare our group to another person's group to see if we are winning or losing. Attendance has always been our way of keeping score. For years it seems like the mantra has been, "The person with the biggest group wins."

Attendance is something we can measure, and we can compare the number to last week's attendance, or attendance last year on the same Sunday, or the attendance of other groups. But is this the primary way we should measure the success of groups? I do believe we should measure attendance, but like the golf scorecard, measuring attendance is like measuring the total number of shots taken. It is a one-dimensional way to see how well you are doing in golf, and it is a one-dimensional way to view your Bible study group. Could there be other ways to measure the effectiveness and success of Bible study groups? I believe the answer is a resounding yes.

Creating a New Measurement Tool for Groups

When I began to focus on improving my golf game, I invested a lot of money in golf shoes, golf clubs, a golf bag (two, actually—a cart bag and a stand bag), buckets of balls, and private lessons. My scoring improved but not in relation to the large cash outlays I made.

As my golf game evolved, I learned there was more to measure than just my total score. I learned about important measurements that could help me improve my game. When I began tracking these things and moved past only being concerned about my score, my golf game improved quickly. I had focused too much on my total score without measuring the things that could actually lower it. I began measuring things like:

- Driving distance (how far the ball travels from the tee box to its resting place).
- GIR (greens in regulation). GIR on a par 3 means hitting the ball onto the green in 1

stroke, 2 or fewer strokes on a par 4, and 3 strokes or fewer on a par 5.

- FIR (fairways in regulation). FIR means hitting the ball into the main landing area on a par 4 or par 5 hole—the place where the grass is cut short.
- Number of putts per round.
- Sand saves (hitting the golf ball out of a sand bunker, onto the green, and making par).

Tracking FIRs, GIRS, putts, driving distance, and sand saves helps me see where I need to work on the weaker aspects of my game. The same is true in the world of Bible study. By creating a new scorecard for groups, we can get a better picture of our performance in leading our groups. This can create a big advantage for group leaders who begin to use a system for tracking their "game."

Creating a New Scorecard for Groups

Earlier I said that the old scorecard for Bible study groups focused on attendance. It is not a *bad* measurement, but it certainly falls short of giving group leaders a complete picture of what is taking place in their groups—or what *should* be taking place. What if we measured groups in ways that might give us a better idea of how Bible study groups are really doing? As with my new golf scorecard, we could see where we need to improve.

It is time to create a new way to measure the success of groups.

The mission of ongoing Bible study groups can be summed up in four measurements. Those four measurements make up the four sections of this book. Together they make up the new scorecard for groups. These four measurements create a new framework for evaluating the success of Bible study groups.

I began using these four goals in my church's Bible study groups years ago when I served as a full-time discipleship pastor. These four measurements keep the focus on what matters most. To say it another way, they help groups know whether they are on target. The four main measurements cover essentials such as Bible study and spiritual growth, evangelism, relationships, and serving others. They are listed below:

- Learn and obey God's Word.
- Invite people to become disciples.
- Form deeper relationships.
- Engage in acts of service.

When I was earning my degree in Christian education, my professors taught "the six pillars of Sunday School"— reach, teach, witness, worship, care, and fellowship. I found a new way to say something similar through the LIFE acrostic. And if you look closely, you'll see all six pillars represented.

Because I believe firmly that there is more to group life than what happens on a Sunday morning, the first letter of each of the four measurements spells the acrostic LIFE. Bible study should not only be about what happens from nine to noon on Sunday; it should prepare Jesus's disciples for a life-time of devotion to Him. We do not attend a Bible study to learn interesting or unique facts about the Bible. We learn the Word of God so that we can obey it. From cradle to grave, the Bible teaches us the way to please God as we love Him with all our heart, mind, soul, and strength.

As we explore each aspect of the LIFE acrostic that makes up the four sections of this book, we will ask four questions related to each of those measurements. That means we will ask sixteen diagnostic questions about the overall practices of Bible study groups. Together these sixteen questions will assist us in measuring the success of groups, giving us a new way to measure how effectively groups are accomplishing the four main LIFE measurements.

No group is going to be able to answer yes to all sixteen questions, and that is all right. We must first be honest about the current state of our groups. Then we can move forward and work to improve them. It may feel a bit daunting at first, but I promise that in time group leaders will have much healthier groups.

In golf, as in Bible study, there is more than one way to measure success. It is time, perhaps past time, to move beyond making attendance the main measurement of group health. We will continue to count people—that won't change. But by asking sixteen key questions related to the four LIFE measurements, groups can be reoriented to a new way of measuring success in Bible study.

How to Use This Book

Review

After reading each chapter, focus on the three main ideas that are listed. These will help you remember the most important ideas from each chapter.

Personal Reflection

Respond to the end-of-chapter discussion questions as you read the book. Consider how you might lead your Bible study group to implement changes that would position it to be more effective in accomplishing the four measurements of group success.

Group Study

Commit to read the book with several others. Read one chapter a week and discuss the concepts at a weekly gathering. Or, to move through the content more quickly, read one section (four chapters) at a time, respond to the reflection questions, and discuss them all at a weekly meeting. Focus on applying the content to your ministry context.

Training

Purchase a copy of the book for each group leader in your church's teaching ministry and ask them to read it prior to a training event you conduct that focuses on the content in the book.

Do

There is a to-do list at the end of each chapter. Accomplish the to-dos as a way of applying the concepts found in each chapter.

Measurement 1

Learn and Obey God's Word

Chapter 1

Are Group Members Growing as Disciples?

My first job was stocking groceries at my local Winn-Dixie supermarket. I remember nervously applying for the job. I was unable to fill out the "prior experience" section of the application because, well, I didn't have any. I had just turned sixteen! As I filled out the application, I thought, *There is no way I'll get hired. I don't have any experience.*

Still, I got an interview with the assistant manager of the grocery store, and afterwards he offered me the job. During my interview he told me he needed to hire several new employees. It turned out that I did have something to offer—a pulse! I am glad he took a chance on me, but when I showed up for my first day of work, I still wondered if I could do the job.

Over time I learned new skills, and I matured in my ability to juggle schoolwork and my new job. The assistant manager was not seeking experience. Instead, he hired people who were eager to work, had a track record of dependability, and could be good team players. The manager was more concerned with character than skills. Those would come with time.

Perhaps you are reading this book and are not currently a group leader in your church's teaching ministry. You might wonder, *Do I have what it takes? Can I help people mature as disciples of Christ?* Those are fair questions, and it means you are taking this leadership role seriously. You may not have a lot of experience, but like the circumstances of my first job, skills can be learned. Maybe you are currently a group leader, but you have questions about whether you are the right person to lead your group and help people grow as disciples.

When God invites someone to serve, He does not necessarily look at their skill level. He looks at their heart. David was Jesse's youngest son and went from herding sheep to leading the nation of Israel as king. When David faced off against Goliath, he was confident in God's ability to win the coming battle. If you had been David, would you have thought, *There's no way I can win against this giant,* or would you have thought, *Goliath is so big, how can I miss!*

Scripture refers to David as "a man after God's own heart" on two occasions. The first is at 1 Samuel 13:14: "The LORD has found a man after his own heart, and the LORD has appointed him as ruler over his people." The second time the phrase was used by the apostle Paul in Acts 13:22: "He raised up David as their king and testified about him, 'I have found David the son of Jesse to be a man after my own heart, who will carry out all my will.'" Was David perfect? Far from it! He loved God, but he also failed at times. Despite his failures, David's desire was to honor and serve God. And God used David in some amazing ways.

Character catches God's attention. We know that He constantly searches the earth to find people who love and honor Him. "For the eyes of the LORD roam throughout the earth to show himself strong for those who are wholeheartedly devoted to him" (2 Chron. 16:9). Skills can be taught, but if character is lacking, skills are irrelevant. I love the story of Jesus's earthly father, Joseph. He is described as a righteous man (not perfect, but his heart was inclined toward God). Joseph was faithful to Mary during their journey toward marriage. He was someone who deeply loved. This was evidenced by his desire to put Mary away quietly rather than shame her publicly. Joseph was also an obedient man.

He immediately did as the angel of the Lord instructed him in a dream. I imagine that God chose Joseph to be Jesus's earthly father in part because of his character. Character matters. You do not have to be perfect, but you should see progress in your walk with God.

> Skills can be taught, but if character is lacking, skills are irrelevant.

You can lead others to learn and live God's Word. Ask yourself if you have the basic traits listed below. If you do, you are positioned well to be used by God to help others grow in their understanding of God's Word and how to live it out daily. Skills can be taught; character is something you already possess.

Faithfulness

The apostle Paul took young Timothy under his wing and invested in him. In Paul's second letter to Timothy, he told this young pastor how to advance the gospel. The "formula" was not difficult to remember. Paul instructed Timothy to take the Word of God that Paul had spoken in his presence and to pass it along to "faithful men who will be able to teach others also" (2 Tim. 2:2). Note that Paul did not tell Timothy to look for charismatic leaders who already had lots of followers. Instead, the single characteristic Timothy was to look for in those who would join him in preaching and teaching the Scriptures was faithfulness.

What does it mean to be a faithful follower of Christ? In short, it means you do what you say you will do. It means you show up when others do not. It means you are steady in your trust in Christ alone as your Savior. It means others can count on you. Even though you may not feel like you have the gifts and experience to guide a group Bible study, do not despair. If God wanted outstanding, world-class communicators, He would have instructed Timothy to look for that kind of person. He did not. Instead, God wants faithful people to join Him in advancing the gospel. If people are faithful, they can learn the skills needed to be effective leaders.

> God wants faithful people to join Him in advancing the gospel. If people are faithful, they can learn the skills needed to be an effective leader.

Humility

Humility is another characteristic group leaders need. It has been said that humility is not thinking less of yourself but thinking of yourself less. I like that definition. It captures the idea that humble people realize their fallen condition, the depth of their sin, and the incredibly deep grace that saved them. Humble people look for ways to serve others, and they put others first. In Jesus's Sermon on the Mount, He reminded us, "Blessed are the humble, for they will inherit the earth" (Matt. 5:5).

Humility was a quality Jesus possessed. In Philippians 2:8 we are told that Jesus "humbled himself by becoming obedient to the point of death—even to death on a cross." James, the half brother of Jesus, encouraged first-century Christians to consider the benefits of humility when he reminded them, "God resists the proud but gives grace to the humble" (James 4:6). Humble people realize how much Jesus has done for them to save them from the penalty of their sins. Humble people serve because Jesus first served them.

Good Reputation

I am sure you know several people who have a good reputation in your church, workplace, or community. A reputation is the sum of a person's words and actions. It is who they really are. If you are looking for an auto mechanic, you want someone known for his good work.

Luke reported that when the early church found itself in a predicament, unable to meet the needs of widows, a plan was formed to enlist men from within the church. "Brothers and sisters, select from among you seven men of good reputation" (Acts 6:3). If you have a good reputation, God can use you as a Bible study leader.

Financial Integrity

Moses found himself in a difficult position. Scripture records that he alone judged the people, and they stood around him from morning until night waiting for him to hear their cases. On most days, people went away without having their cases heard because there were just too many cases for one man to judge. Moses's father-in-law Jethro arrived on the scene in Exodus 18 and offered Moses some great advice: "But you should select from all the people able men, God-fearing, trustworthy, and *hating dishonest profit*. Place them over the people as commanders of thousands, hundreds, fifties, and tens" (Exod. 18:21, emphasis added).

It is no surprise that Moses selected leaders who were God-fearing and trustworthy, but Jethro added another qualifier: "hating dishonest profit." This was important for people who would soon be in positions to judge cases. They would need to have a strong moral compass that could say no to bribes. Financial integrity is important for God's leaders today as well. We must act generously toward those who have financial needs, pay our debts, manage resources, and pay our employees. We should avoid even the appearance of evil. Many ministries have been ruined by the love of money.

God-Fearer

Solomon was the wisest man ever to walk the earth. He asked God for wisdom to lead his people, and God granted that request. When Solomon wrote the Old Testament book of Ecclesiastes, he compared the ways of unbelievers and God-fearers when he wrote, "Although a sinner does evil a hundred times and prolongs his life, I also know that it will go well with God-fearing people, for they are reverent before him" (Eccles. 8:12).

The fear of God is seen in Scripture as a healthy reverence and respect for Him. It is a realization on the part of God's highest creation, man, that although he was made a little lower than angels, he is not God. God is perfect, powerful, and mighty. God-fearing believers realize how precariously they were perched before God rescued them. He saved them from an eternity apart from Him. God's people fear Him but not because they are afraid of Him, nor are they fearful of experiencing His wrath. Rather, God's people fear Him because they realize the magnitude of His great power.

Imperfect People

Perhaps this is the best news of all. God uses imperfect people to accomplish His will. He can even use people whose character is deeply flawed. In our weakness His strength is made perfect. No pastor, Sunday school teacher, deacon, or committee member has ever been perfect. Only one man in history can claim that honor, and His name is Jesus. If you have ever said to yourself, *I've failed too much for God to use me*, then you are exactly the kind of person He often chooses. Consider the people He used throughout the Bible to accomplish His will. None were perfect. Some were far from it:

> The fear of God is seen in Scripture as a healthy reverence and respect for Him. It is a realization on the part of God's highest creation, man, that although he was made a little lower than angels, he is not God.

- Moses was a drunk.
- Jonah ran from God.
- Elijah was depressed and wanted to die.
- Rahab was a prostitute.
- David was a murderer and an adulterer.
- Peter denied knowing Jesus and ran away at a crucial moment.

- Paul was the archenemy of the church, a persecutor, and a murderer.
- And there are countless others!

If we want people to learn and live God's Word, they will need group leaders to guide them. No group leader will ever be perfect, but God will use people whose hearts are committed to him (2 Chron. 16:9). As you grow as a disciple, you can help others walk that same spiritual pathway. You do not have to be perfect.

What Signs of Growth Should I See?

My grandson Logan is now three and a half years old. Before he was born, he captivated our hearts. As a baby, he cooed and smiled when we babbled. And yes, he also ate, spit up, burped, slept, and did all the things infants do in their first months of life.

When he made it to three and a half years, he was much different. He did not look the same as he did three years prior. His vocabulary has grown tremendously. When he finds something funny, he throws his head back and laughs, smiling from ear to ear. He puts sentences together and conveys his thoughts. He has learned some nice motor skills and can swing a plastic golf club, throw balls, run, jump, play on his swing set, and feed himself. He has learned to recite his ABCs and count numbers in order. He's learned his name, his birthday, and the name of the town in which he lives. He has even learned a little mischief along the way. I know Logan is maturing because I can *see* that he is maturing. I can point to specific things he is able to do that he could not do a few years ago.

In a similar way, God's people show signs of growth. There are research-validated indicators, "signposts" if you will, that a believer is growing and maturing in Christ. These signposts of discipleship are much like trail signs in the woods. When you go for a hike, you see signposts that tell you how far you are from the next significant place on the trail. The signposts help you know that you are making progress, that you are still on the right path.

As stated earlier, attendance is one way to measure a Bible study group. In fact, attendance has been the primary measurement on the old scorecard for groups. But what if group leaders began asking, "Are my group members growing as disciples?" What if group leaders looked to see if their teaching was making a difference in people's lives as seen through the spiritual growth of the group members? The Great Commission tells us to make disciples, and one sign we are successful is that they learn to obey (Matt. 28:18–20).

Signposts of Discipleship

What if it were possible to know if Christians were making progress in their walks with Jesus? The Transformational Discipleship project discovered how believers grow. It was the largest research project about discipleship ever undertaken. Conducted by Lifeway Research, the Transformational Discipleship project discovered that disciples grow and mature in eight key areas. In the original research, these were known as the eight attributes of discipleship. Today we like referring to these as the eight signposts of discipleship.

Dr. Philip Nation, who coauthored the book *Transformational Discipleship* with Michael Kelley and Eric Geiger, had these helpful words to say about the eight attributes (signposts) of discipleship.

In the church, our work is to see disciples made. But can you really "measure" discipleship? A strong case can be made that it is ludicrous to measure transformation in a person's life. Nevertheless, there are biblical injunctions that halt our progress into sin and prescriptions that lead us toward spiritual maturity. In the Transformational Discipleship project, we did not set out to randomly create objective measurements against which a person's life would be deemed infantile, growing, or mature. We did, however, uncover attributes that indicate growth and/or the desire that growth is occurring. The research revealed eight issues we named the "Attributes of Discipleship." They are not new ideas necessarily, but they stand out as key ideas in the lives of Protestants in North America.

> *Bible Engagement.* It should go without saying that believers will be engaged in the study of the Scriptures. Leadership, however, must often begin with the restatement of the obvious. Transformation can be recognized in a person when their mind is sharpened by the Bible, their perspective is shaped by the Bible, and their actions are directed by the Bible.

> *Obeying God and Denying Self.* Discipleship is the process of obedience to one who is in authority over you. In our study, we found that people progressing in their faith are the ones who prioritize God's desires over self-will. Transformation can be seen in them because they progressively set aside earthly delights for kingdom priorities.

> *Serving God and Others.* Just as Jesus said that He had come to serve and not be served, so must believers. The choice to serve others is just that . . . a choice. It highlights a maturity

of soul that we allow the needs of others to trump our own needs. Transformation is evident when personal needs, and even dreams, are set aside for the needs we see in others.

Sharing Christ. Inherent to being a disciple of Christ is the making of other disciple-makers for Christ. Even with the need to live out the effects of the gospel, maturing believers know that speaking about the message is a necessity. Transformation is evident when we talk about the source of it.

Exercising Faith. Can you measure a person's faith? Probably not. But you can see it when it is put into action. Believers participating in the research noted that they knew the importance of living by faith as opposed to by personal strength. Transformation is seen in believers when risk-aversion is set aside, and our lives are characterized by faithful obedience to God's will.

Seeking God. A person becomes a disciple of Christ because they intend to follow Him and become like Him. A continuous hunger should arise from this life. It is referred to in Scripture as our "first love," and believers are commanded at times to return to it. Transformation is seen when our desire is to know God more deeply and experience His work more fully.

Building Relationships. Our faith is personal, but it is not intended to be private. Jesus established the church for our collective good and our collective growth. After all, humans are relational by nature. As believers, our horizontal relationships should develop just as our vertical relationship with God does. Transformation is occurring when relational maturity is evident in our lives.

Unashamed. From previous studies, "unashamed" was new to our list, but we were not surprised by its appearance in the research. It is natural to think that a person following Christ would be willing to publicize such a matter. The research noted that believers felt it appropriate, and even necessary, for others to know them as Christians and be held accountable for a life exemplary of that name. Transformation is evident when a believer is unashamed in presenting their own life as being aligned with Christ.[1]

As we consider the first measurement of groups, *Learn and obey God's Word*, we must ask an initial question: "Are group members showing signs of maturing in Christ?" Are people in our groups:

- *Engaging with their Bibles?* Are group members engaging in daily quiet times and personal daily studies? Is God speaking to group members as they spend time in His Word?
- *Obeying God and denying self?* Are people living for God or for themselves?
- *Serving God and others?* Are people leaving the group to become leaders in other

ministries in the church? Do they meet the needs of people in their community?

- *Sharing Christ?* Are people in Bible study groups sharing their testimonies and the gospel with others?
- *Exercising faith?* Are people faithfully following God's will instead of living in fear and being risk averse?
- *Seeking God?* Are people attending the group? Participating in worship? Plugging into the life of the church? Participating in discipleship courses and mentoring relationships?
- *Building relationships?* How deep are the relationships group members have with one another? With fellow church members? With people far from God spiritually?
- *Living unashamed?* Are group members reticent about letting others know they follow Jesus, or are they proud to be Christian?

Creating the New Scorecard for Groups

As we wrap up this chapter, let's start creating a new scorecard for groups that measures more than just attendance. When I play a round of golf, I keep my score on my own scorecard (they are designed for up to four people to track their scores during a round). I keep track of my score on each hole, but below that line I write FIR, GIR, Putts, and SS (sand save) on the remaining lines where I would normally track the scores of the group. This way I can look after the round is over and see which area of my game needs the most improvement. Then it's off to the practice area before I head home.

The first goal of a group is to *Learn and Obey God's Word*. Learning God's Word should lead to living God's Word. How is your group doing? Be honest! Based on the eight signposts of discipleship we just read, would you say your people are walking the discipleship pathway? Are they growing as disciples? Can you see the eight signposts of discipleship in their daily lives? Rate your group below. I realize you may have people in your group who are growing and others who are not growing as much. Think about the group *as a whole*: Are the members showing evidence of the eight signposts in their walks with Jesus? What grade would you give them?

NEW SCORECARD FOR GROUPS				
		GRADE		
	LEARN AND OBEY GOD'S WORD	**A**	**B**	**C**	**D**
1	**Are group members growing as disciples?**				
2					
3					
4					

In the chapters ahead, we will add to this scorecard, and we will ultimately have a new one that will evaluate a Bible study group by asking sixteen different questions. Remember, we are looking at four main measurements of groups with four questions related to each one that will help us determine if Bible study groups are postured for success.

Main Ideas

1. There is more to measuring the success of a Bible study group than just the attendance of the members. Attendance

is important but not necessarily the way to observe the health of a group.

2. People need group leaders to help them learn and apply God's Word. It is important not only to teach the Bible accurately but also to help people rightly apply it to life.

3. God uses imperfect group leaders to guide His people. God desires group leaders to be people who are righteous (not perfect but saved) and striving to be people of good character and reputation. The skills that are needed to teach and lead will be learned along the way.

Questions for Discussion

1. Besides attendance, how do group leaders, group members, and others evaluate the effectiveness of Bible study groups?

2. Why do we often view attendance as the primary measurement for group health?

3. If group leaders and group members began using spiritual maturity as a measurement, how might that change the overall nature of groups?

To-Do List

1. Evaluate yourself using the eight signposts of discipleship. Which ones are present in your walk with Christ?

2. Among those signposts, pick two that you rated lower than the others. What practical steps can you take to strengthen these as you move forward?

3. Review the characteristics of people God has used to lead His people. Which one is your greatest characteristic? Which is the weakest? How could you make the weakest characteristic a stronger part of who you are in Christ? What changes need to be made?

Chapter 2

Are Bible Studies Well Prepared and Engaging?

I grew up in the Dallas-Fort Worth metroplex. I, of course, became a fan of the Dallas Cowboys at an early age (don't hate). Tom Landry was the first coach of the Dallas Cowboys and was known to be a committed Christian. He had a long and successful career with the Cowboys and believed in preparation. He led the Cowboys to win multiple Super Bowls during his time as the head coach.

Landry knew that what took place *before* the game led to success *during* the game. A player, or a team, could have a strong will to win, but without adequate preparation, a strong will would not be enough to assure a victory. To win at football, Landry understood that players and coaches had to be willing to put in time for practice and preparation. Plays had to be memorized. Game film had to be analyzed, and hundreds of practice plays had to be run weekly. What does this have to do with Bible study? Plenty.

Proverbs 21:31 has become one of my favorite verses. It says, "A horse is prepared for the day of battle, but victory comes from the LORD." Don't you love that? Let's discuss what led the writer to say this. Before troops went into battle, they trained. They fashioned weapons and developed strategies. The troops who rode horses were also tasked with training those animals. The battlefield was a noisy, confusing place. Horses needed equipment that fit them, but they also needed to be ready for the chaos of battle. Before horses and soldiers stepped onto the battlefield, endless hours of preparation had already taken place. "A horse is prepared for the day of battle" means that from the human side of the equation, people prepared. The soldiers did not just show up for battle without practicing, preparing, and planning. The soldiers did what they could to partner with God—they prepared, but the writer of Proverbs 21:31 made sure to remind readers that even though preparation is important, having God at your side is crucial.

Let's apply this to a Bible study group. Teacher A had a busy week. Work consumed his daytime hours, and he coached his kid's soccer team two nights this week and also had a game on Saturday afternoon. By Saturday night, he is exhausted from the activities of the week. He is a Bible study teacher at his church, and he has not looked at his group's Bible study yet. He only has an hour to look over his lesson before bedtime, but he reasons that he can review it first thing on Sunday morning. He thinks to himself, *I'm doing the best I can. After all, I'm a volunteer.*

Teacher B, however, has taken a different approach. He studied his lesson a little every day this week. He's read some biblical commentary in his leader materials, crafted a teaching plan, prayed for his group members, and even found a current event that tied to the Bible study; he is going to use that to generate interest. He is convinced that God has spoken to him this week and is excited to guide his group to study God's Word. He can hardly wait for Sunday!

Which of these two group leaders has a Proverbs 21:31 mindset? Obviously, Teacher B is the winner. He knows that he is responsible to prepare well, not just show up and "hope for the best." But how many group leaders show up on Sunday morning, hoping God will make up for their lack of preparation?

Group leaders have discovered that effective preparation is foundational in creating engaging Bible studies. By "engaging," I mean a Bible study in which the group members are pulled into the world of the biblical writer. An engaging Bible study can invite group members to see the Scripture in a way that makes it come to life, a way that says, "This is relevant for me today." Engaging Bible studies encourage group members to talk—to share their thoughts about the text, to share their stories, and to become more open and vulnerable. Engaging Bible studies always lead to practical ways to apply the text to life. Engaging studies incorporate the eight learning approaches so that people's learning preferences are met over time.

> How many group leaders show up on Sunday morning, hoping God will make up for their lack of preparation?

Churches often invite me to train their group leaders on Sunday afternoons. When I travel and train on location at a church, I like to sit in a Bible study group that morning. I do not typically share where I work or what I do. I simply participate; I am a guest that day. In most groups the Bible study is less than an engaging one. Here is what I normally experience:

The group leader stands behind a podium or sits behind a small desk.

The room is arranged in rows (more on this later).

Once the Bible study begins, the group leader does most of the talking.

Group members do a lot of listening.

The group leader asks questions, but they tend to be text based, which most people do not answer.

The group leader tends to answer his own questions because of the lack of response.

Was the group leader prepared? Yes. In most cases the person leading the study has a good grasp of the Scripture. But the group's study centers on him, not the group members. It does not inspire people to be consistent in their attendance, nor does it give them confidence to invite friends to the group. Preparation is important, highly important, and equally indispensable is the engagement of the group members in the study.

> Effectiveness in leading a Bible study is related to the level of preparation a group leader is willing to undertake.

Effectiveness in leading a Bible study is related to the level of preparation a group leader is willing to undertake. If a boxer cheats during his training time, cutting corners and finishing his daily training early, the lack of preparation will become evident under the bright lights of the ring. Bible study leaders understand this, too. Preparation, or a lack of it, will always be revealed during the Bible study. If a teacher cheats throughout the week and chooses not to prepare well, it will be evident soon enough.

Eating the Elephant

Here is a simple schedule that can help you lead consistently good Bible studies (this schedule assumes that Bible study takes place on Sunday). If you teach on another day of the week, simply modify the schedule to fit your context. Preparing a Bible study is a serious task, and it is made more difficult if the group leader starts the process later rather than sooner. You know the adage about eating an elephant: you do it one bite at a time. It's the same with Bible study preparation. It is easier if you bite off a little bit each day instead of trying to take it all in in one sitting.

The schedule below is the one I prefer, and it only takes thirty minutes a day. Some of you could adopt this and prepare on your lunch hour. Others of you could set aside time each evening to prepare. If you are willing to give up a television show that lasts thirty minutes and use that time to prepare your group's Bible study, you will experience a new level of confidence as a group leader. For a Bible study leader, there is no worse feeling than walking into a Bible study knowing you are underprepared.

Monday

- Read the lesson passage, but this time in different translations (NASB, KJV, HCSB, NIV, ESV). Take note of how certain words are sometimes translated differently. Look them up in a Bible dictionary and understand the meaning of the words in their original languages.

- Jot down any themes you see in the passage.

Tuesday

- Identify key words and concepts, Bible characters, and places mentioned in the passage.
- Consult commentaries, your Bible study series' leader guide, a Bible atlas, a Bible dictionary, or other resources to help you know more about the people, places, and customs mentioned in the Bible passage.

Wednesday

- Read the lesson passage again, asking these application questions of the text:
    - Is there an attitude to adjust?
    - Is there a promise to claim?
    - Is there a priority to change?
    - Is there a lesson to learn?
    - Is there an issue to resolve?
    - Is there a command to obey?
    - Is there an activity to stop or start?
    - Is there a truth to believe?
    - Is there a sin to confess?
    - Is there an example to follow?

Thursday

- Review your curriculum's leader guide and the suggested teaching plan.

- As you continue to review the suggested teaching plan, add or delete steps to fit your group and the amount of time you have for Bible study.

Friday

- Finalize your teaching plan.

Saturday

- Review your teaching plan.
- Gather any supplies you need for the group Bible study.

Saturday Night

- Go to bed on time and be well rested for tomorrow's ministry to your group.

Sunday Morning

- Get to church early.
- Prepare your room.
- Greet and interact with people as they arrive.
- Start on time.
- End on time.

Sunday Afternoon

- Reflect on what happened during your Bible study that morning. What worked? What didn't work? What will you do differently next time?
- Read next week's Bible study passage at least twice. Meditate on the words and let them soak into your mind and heart. Do not do

any detailed study at this time; just read the passage you will teach next time.

- Pray for God to speak to you through His Word as you prepare to guide your group's next session.
- Pray for insight and wisdom into your group members and the way the Scripture passage intersects their lives. Think about how your group members might apply the Word to their lives.

Prepare with Group Members in Mind

The Gospels contain many stories of large crowds that followed Jesus. I cannot speak for you, but when I am in a sea of people, I see a crowd of people. When Jesus was surrounded by crowds, He often saw individuals. The Scripture records:

> There was a man named Zacchaeus who was a chief tax collector, and he was rich. He was trying to see who Jesus was, but he was not able because of the crowd, since he was a short man. So running ahead, he climbed up a sycamore tree to see Jesus, since he was about to pass by that way. When Jesus came to the place, he looked up and said to him, "Zacchaeus, hurry and come down because today it is necessary for me to stay at your house." (Luke 19:2–5)

Another time, a large crowd pressed in around Jesus, and a woman reached out and touched the hem of His garment. Jesus immediately focused His attention on her when He felt power go out from Him (Luke 8:42b–48). He focused on just one individual in the crowd. The woman approached Jesus, trembling. He told her that her faith had healed her and to go in peace.

These two stories provide encouragement to me as I prepare Bible studies for my group. Instead of seeing "the crowd" (the entire group), I like to see one or two individuals. As group leaders prepare their Bible studies, they should consider how a specific group member might benefit from the passage that will be studied. If group leaders get to know their group members as individuals, they will learn their hobbies, their personalities, their passions, and their stories. Group

> I cannot speak for you, but when I am in a sea of people, I see a crowd of people. When Jesus was surrounded by crowds, He often saw individuals.

leaders will learn about their backgrounds from childhood and beyond. They will learn about their fears, hopes, and aspirations. Group leaders will discover the unanswered questions that often plague their people, and group leaders will identify ways in which group members need to exercise their faith so they grow into more fully devoted followers of Christ.

When group leaders begin to see individuals and not just the crowd, they will find themselves tailoring the group's studies to help individuals mature in Christ. Rather than simply presenting a Bible study, group leaders begin to serve as guides. Guides know the destination they want individuals to reach because they know their people. Group leaders should see the faces of individuals as they prepare the group's

> When group leaders begin to see individuals and not just the crowd, they will find themselves tailoring the group's studies to help individuals mature in Christ.

study. They should know that on a particular Sunday, they have addressed a need in the life of one or more of their group members.

If group leaders see individuals and not just the crowd, they will find that they are able to accelerate life transformations among their group members. Those group members will begin showing evidence that they are maturing in the eight attributes (signposts) of discipleship I mentioned in the preceding chapter.

Prepare Using Study Tools

I love tools. While I'm writing this, my son, Ryan, is in college. He works part-time at a national home improvement store. I can spend hours wandering through that hardware store without ever getting bored. There are tools for everything! No matter what the job is, someone has created a tool to help get the job done. If you want to make me happy, give me a gift card to a hardware store for my birthday, and I will find a new tool to add to my growing collection of tools that now line my garage wall.

I encourage group leaders to build a library of Bible study tools. Just like hardware tools, specific Bible study tools help group leaders accomplish specific jobs. If you are a group leader, don't rush out and buy all of these at one time. You may want to invest in a digital platform such as Logos. It is the one I use because it contains so many helpful study tools.

You can find any of the following at my company's website, lifeway.com.

Bible Dictionary

A Bible dictionary is a basic tool that every group leader needs in his or her library. This tool is designed to give you information about people, places, and customs. Bible dictionaries typically include references to the original words from languages such as Greek, Hebrew, and Aramaic. Bible dictionaries have verse references where the words are found so that words can be studied in context. In biblical study, context is key.

Atlas

A Bible atlas is another valuable study tool that all group leaders should have in their libraries. Your Bible may contain a set of maps in the back, or maps may be placed throughout the Bible, but a Bible atlas is much more exhaustive and provides hundreds of maps that will not be found in most study Bibles.

Concordance

A concordance lists words found in the Bible in alphabetical order with verse references. If you look up the word *love*, you will find all the references to that word found in your Bible (concordances are translation specific, so you will want a concordance from the same translation of Scripture as your Bible). An "exhaustive" concordance is much larger than a normal concordance. The difference is that in the exhaustive concordance, every reference of a word is listed, not just a few of them.

Commentary

A commentary is often a group leader's best friend. A commentary is just what it sounds like—an author's comments on a book, or books, of the Bible. Commentaries tend to be translation specific as well, but not always. A good commentary will provide you with an outline of a book of the Bible, and it will include verse-by-verse comments by the author to help you understand the nuances in the biblical text. Commentaries range from those that are in "everyday speak" to those that are technical (some of the more advanced commentaries include Hebrew and Greek words without any definition; they assume the reader understands those languages). Because of this, be careful when you purchase a commentary; make sure it fits your level of learning. The last thing we want is for you to drown in jargon.

Prepare the Meeting Place

If your teaching ministry is at your church's campus, your Bible study group meets in a room. One of the truisms of a ministry like Sunday school is that "the room speaks." The arrangement of chairs, the placement of the group leader's teaching position—it all communicates something about the way the group will be guided through a Bible study. It also communicates a lot about what is expected from group members during the study.

Let's consider several ways to arrange rooms, plus the pros and cons of each. I have a favorite, but that will come later. Remember, one of the goals of groups is to engage people in Bible study. You will want to find a room arrangement that does that. When participation is maximized, the Bible comes alive. If your current room arrangement does not provide an engaging, and ultimately transforming environment, then it may be time to rearrange it. Which of the scenarios below best describes your room?

The Classroom Model

This room arrangement is the most common one I see in churches. The room is arranged like a public-school classroom. It has an "academic" feel. When you enter a room arranged like this, it says something (remember, the room speaks). A room arranged like this says to the group member or guest, "The teacher is in charge. He is the expert. You are here to listen. The teacher has many important things to tell you."

A room arrangement like this does not boost discussion. If I am a member of a group whose room is arranged like this, I spend most of the time looking at the back of someone's head. Because the teaching is centered at the front of the room, group members must listen carefully and keep their minds from wandering. They are not given much opportunity to interact with the group leader or the members of the group. It is a great room arrangement for auditory learners but not for everyone else.

This model also indicates the major goal of the group is biblical exposition. This is not necessarily bad. We are supposed to learn the Scripture! Paul reminded Timothy, "From infancy you have known the sacred Scriptures, which are able to give you wisdom for salvation through faith in Christ Jesus" (2 Tim. 3:15). The challenge with this room model, however, is that teaching tends to become the pinnacle of group life. A room arrangement like this sometimes discourages the group from looking outward for new members and for people who are far from God because the goal of the group has become "to go deeper."

The Banquet Model

When a group meets around tables, good things happen. Meeting around circular tables ensures that people see one another's faces. Seeing faces jump-starts conversations and discussion. When you attend a banquet, a workplace meeting, a wedding, or other type of event, round tables are often used because food, fellowship, and conversation are important elements in those venues.

During a Bible study, round tables give people a place to rest their Bibles, coffee cups, and other items. Tables also naturally put people into smaller groups. These are all good things. Personally, I like the convenience and benefits of round tables.

A caution should be made, however, about using round tables. While they have advantages, they do come with a cost. Tables are an added expense, and they quickly take up much floor space in a room, limiting the number of people who can attend the group's Bible study. Most buildings with classrooms have been built at a cost of about $150 to $200 per square foot. One six-foot round table takes up just over twenty-eight square feet of space. When the cost of construction per foot is multiplied by $175 (the average of the two previous construction costs), a single table rests on top of $4,900 of classroom space! If a room has four tables, a group has used almost $20,000 of space for coffee cups and Bibles. In addition, the room will hold more people if they sit in chairs without tables. Once Bible study groups begin using tables, it is hard to go back, so be cautious. Make sure you understand the benefits and the costs of this model.

The Conference Model

This is a room arrangement I see from time to time. Tables are used to create a U shape, and group members can see one another's faces. This helps boost discussion in ways the classroom model does not. It also allows the group leader to walk among his or her group members because of the open-ended arrangement of the tables. I have seen some Bible study leaders use a laptop and PowerPoint slideshow to present an engaging study using this kind of room arrangement. The same challenges from the banquet model are in play with this scenario. Tables take up valuable floor space that cost thousands of dollars to build. You will have to weigh the pros and cons before adopting this as your group's model.

The Living Room Model

Spoiler alert! This is my favorite room arrangement! I have used this in every group my wife and I have led. This model puts everyone in a circle, looking at one another but without the costs and limitations of round tables. This is what would happen if my group met in my home. We would sit on couches and chairs in the main part of my house. I can duplicate that feeling in an on-campus room by arranging my room like this.

This room arrangement speaks volumes. Because I sit among my group members, it communicates that I am a fellow learner, not necessarily the "expert" in the group who stands over them to teach. The room arrangement boosts discussion and jump-starts relationships in ways that do not happen when people's chairs are arranged in rows. Because there are no tables, I can maximize the number of people who can be members of the group, and I am not placing tables on top of thousands of dollars of expensive education space.

Each of the above ways to arrange your classroom in an on-campus setting has pros and cons. Talk with your pastor or staff leader who is responsible for your church's teaching ministry and determine which one is best for your context.

Prepare by Using Ongoing Studies

When I served two churches in Texas, and long before I accepted a leadership position at Lifeway to manage the adult ongoing Bible studies (ongoing studies are designed for groups that meet every week), I guided both churches to use ongoing studies in all their Sunday morning groups. No one had to tell me the advantages and strengths of ongoing Bible studies. I learned that while on the job.

When I first arrived, the second church I served allowed groups to choose any kind of Bible studies they desired. Some used ongoing studies, while others used short-term, closed group studies (these kinds of studies are not easily joined after the second meeting of the group). Other groups used nothing at all because the group leaders preferred creating their own studies each week.

In time I was able to move all adult groups to use the same ongoing Bible study series. The group leaders commented how easy it was to use ongoing studies to prepare their weekly studies because of the large amount of helps available to them. Using ongoing studies provides numerous ways to help the group leader as well as the group members:

- **Time is saved.** Group leaders are typically some of the busiest people in the church. The last thing they need is to prepare a Bible study from scratch every week. That time is better used in relating to group members and guests. An ongoing curriculum series saves time because of the biblical commentary, teaching plans, and other helps that give group leaders ways to explain the biblical text and engage their group members in Bible study effectively.

- **Trustworthiness is guaranteed.** Because ongoing studies are created by men and women with expertise in theology and Christian education, group leaders can trust that they are receiving outstanding and accurate information about the biblical text. If group leaders conduct their own research online, they may not know whether the data they discover is accurate. They can also inadvertently pass along inaccurate information to their group members. The vetting processes with Christian publishers like Lifeway ensure that trustworthiness is always achieved.

> Because ongoing studies are created by men and women with expertise in theology and Christian education, group leaders can trust that they are receiving outstanding and accurate information about the biblical text.

- **Creativity is enhanced.** Session teaching plans are created by people who have advanced degrees and lead groups themselves.

These men and women understand how people learn. They recommend ideas for leading group members to study the Bible in engaging and creative ways. Because we all do not learn the same way, a variety of teaching activities are needed to maximize people's involvement. If group leaders create their own studies, they tend to default to one or two ways of teaching that they prefer (not necessarily how the people in the group prefer to learn).

- **Balance is assured.** Ongoing studies ensure that balanced discipleship takes place. Studies are often rotated between Old and New Testament books. Different biblical genres are considered when a Bible study series is created. It is not uncommon to find that Christian publishers like Lifeway have balanced studies between books of the Bible that include genres like prophecy, poetry, and history. In addition to those genres, consideration is given to books like the Gospels, the Epistles, and books of wisdom and poetry. All of this happens when the studies are created. This means that group leaders never have to think about the time-consuming and detailed process of balancing studies over time. Instead, by using an ongoing Bible study series, group leaders experience increased time to serve their groups and prepare their studies.

- **Apprentice leaders are developed.** Another crucial preparation that must take place in Bible study groups is the development of future leaders. This happens when a group leader hands his apprentice the same materials he uses to prepare the group's Bible studies. New groups are always needed, and when an apprentice teacher is enlisted, his confidence increases because he has ongoing study materials to guide his preparation. I will discuss this more in an upcoming chapter on developing apprentice leaders.

Preparation Helps Pace the Bible Study

Do you remember the story of the tortoise and the hare? It is one of Aesop's fables and has been read by millions of children and adults. In the story, two unequal competitors agree to a race. The hare quickly runs ahead of the slower tortoise and stops to take a nap. The short burst of energy on the part of the hare did not prove to be wise. The victory went to the tortoise who paced himself and became the unlikely winner. Is there a lesson for Bible study group leaders in this story? Absolutely.

Some group leaders tend to "run fast" through a Bible study, mistakenly thinking they must "get through all the points." That is not the goal! The goal is to make fully mature disciples. As a group leader prepares the

> Some group leaders tend to "run fast" through a Bible study, mistakenly thinking they must "get through all the points." That is not the goal! The goal is to make fully mature disciples.

Bible study, consideration must be given to the time available to the group (in many cases, thirty to forty minutes of actual study time is normal). This available time must be weighed against the content to be covered in a single session. In a three-point Bible study, group leaders need to give themselves permission to go slower and spend more time on a single point if necessary. That may be what the Holy Spirit wants the group leader to do from time to time.

Pacing a Bible study is both an art and a science. The average group has between thirty and forty minutes for Bible study, and there are multiple stages in a Bible study. Typical pacing would look like this in a group that has forty minutes for Bible study:

- *Motivation Stage*, 5 minutes. The group leader creates interest in the study by telling a story, showing a video, asking a question, or connecting the study to a current event.
- *Examination Stage*, 25 minutes. The group leader guides an engaging study using a variety of methods.
- *Application Stage*, 10 minutes. The group leader helps people find ways to apply the study immediately. The last thing people want is a history lesson. They want a study that is engaging and can be applied in their everyday lives.

Variety Creates Engagement

I am sure you have heard the phrase, "Variety is the spice of life." I can verify that variety is a good thing. For instance, I enjoy eating at restaurants where I have never been before.

I like vacationing in different places. I get bored by playing the same golf courses repeatedly.

Group members are no different. They enjoy variety in the classroom, but group leaders often fail to "shake things up a bit." Predictability is not our friend when it comes to studying God's Word. Group members need to be kept slightly off balance. They need to come to each Bible study with the question, *I wonder what's going to happen today?* in the forefront of their minds. Predictability gives people yet another excuse not to attend a group's Bible study. It also gives them a reason not to invite others to experience their group's Bible study.

Baseball teams would never send in a pitcher and tell him to throw only one kind of pitch. The opposing team would soon hit every ball into the outfield bleachers! Nor would a football team run the same plays down after down. Pitchers throw changeups, and football coaches run different plays from their playbooks for a reason. Variety is a must in sports, and variety is needed in Bible study groups, as well. There are some easy ways group leaders can add variety to the Bible study experience.

Vary the Room Arrangement. If a group typically sits in rows, move things around and sit in a circle. Face a different focal wall, too, by moving the chairs around to face a different direction.

Vary the Teaching Methods. Jesus used more than twenty different ways to teach. Modern research has demonstrated that people learn differently, and there are eight ways that people assimilate content. Each of us has a preferred method we enjoy.

Vary the Order of Things. If your group normally begins with prayer, place it at the end. If you end with announcements, start with them.

People Learn Differently

Lifeway has taught group leaders about the eight learning approaches through conferences, books, and webinars. If you have not seen these before, I have listed them below. I look at this list often as I prepare to teach. I ask myself, *Which method(s) have I not used in a while?*

Group leaders must be careful as they prepare their Bible study lessons. One of the easiest traps to fall into is teaching the same way we prefer to learn. I am a "logical/visual" learner; those are the top two ways I prefer to learn. They also tend to be the way I teach. If I am not careful, I will use those two methods over and over and will never connect with the members of my group that do not prefer to learn in those ways.

While leading a Bible study group recently, I realized I had fallen into the trap of teaching by using only a few of the eight learning approaches (the ones I like and prefer). I made an intentional effort to use music in the next Bible study session (it is not one of my favorites!). That next study happened to be about life in the home and was a study from Ephesians 5. I downloaded John Denver's famous song "Country Roads" to my smartphone. I then connected my phone to a Bluetooth speaker. When my group members arrived for our study one Sunday, they entered our room and heard John Denver singing that popular song. Before long the entire group was singing, swaying, and smiling. I asked an open-ended question to tie the music to our upcoming study that morning: "What are your favorite memories about home?" People told stories, some teared up, and others enjoyed reminiscing. That springboarded our group into the study about what the Bible says about life in our homes—what relationships should be between husbands, wives, and children so they rightly relate to one another.

When the study ended, one group member, a woman named Jackie, made the comment, "This was the best Bible study ever!" I did not think it was my best. It was good, but I did not consider it to be a home run. But then I realized that the music connected Jackie to the lesson in ways it did not for me. She was the only member of our group who served as a member of the choir. Jackie was and is a musical learner. I simply used a communication method that resonated with her. Variety matters! It mattered that day to Jackie. And it reminded me of the great need to serve group members by varying my teaching so that all of my group members get to experience Bible study in a way that appeals to them.

To help you understand the eight learning approaches and ways to incorporate them into Bible studies, I have listed a summary of them below. Ask yourself, *Which of these describes the way I like to be taught?* If you lead a group, ask yourself a second question, *Which of these learning approaches have I used over the last thirty days?* I am confident you will discover that you keep going back to the same ones over and over. If that is the case, commit to using some new ones as you guide people to engage with the Bible. You'll see the eight learning approaches followed by a description of the characteristics of people who enjoy that specific strategy. I've also listed a few of the ways group leaders can teach so that engagement is increased.

The Eight Learning Approaches

1. Relational. Relational people are social. They make friends easily and may be good speakers, "people persons." *Methods.* These methods could be case studies, small groups, personal sharing, testimonies, storytelling, debate, interviews, discussion, biblical simulation, dialogue, role-plays, skit, games, brainstorming, and problem solving that depends on others.

2. Verbal. These members learn best through words— reading, writing, speaking, listening. They even enjoy the sounds of words.

Methods. These could be in the form of lectures, question-answer, brainstorming, case study, resource persons, listening teams, personal sharing, oral reading, debate, interview, writing words for songs, monologue, dialogue, paraphrase Scripture, storytelling, panel, skit, games.

3. Visual. Some choose to do exercises that "create their own pictures" and visuals of what they are learning, "see" in their imaginations if no concrete visual.

Methods. These could be videos, movie clips, posters, charts, maps, object lessons, asking "what if" questions, watching drama, collage, drawing diagrams, wire, or paper sculpture.

4. Reflective. These individuals understand who they are and how they feel. They are also comfortable with periods of quiet.

Methods. They thrive on lecture, case study, question-answer, open-ended sentences, attitude scale, creative writing, diary or journal, listening guides, worksheets and study guides, written tests, listening to music, and opinionnaire.

5. Logical. These types enjoy problem solving and reason through difficult situations or rely on analogies.

Methods. Logical exercises could come in the form of written tests, lecture, worksheets or study guides, notebook, outline, word study, statistics, debate, panel, questions that help discern relationships.

6. Physical. Physical group members are active, have good coordination, play out a story, and enjoy hands-on activities.

Methods. Providing opportunities to provide mobility is important. This could look like moving to agree/disagree poster, joining hands in a circle, art activities (wire/paper sculpture, paper tearing, painting, etc.) arranging room, games, singing with motions, biblical simulation, skit role play.

7. Musical. These people enjoy music, tend to be good listeners, and find it easy to express themselves through music.

Methods. Writing words for well-known pieces of music relating to the lesson, comparing words of hymns to Scripture, or listening to recorded music (sacred or secular).

8. Natural. These people are explorers. They enjoy the beauty, investigation, and exploration of God's creation.

Methods. Collect or display items from nature, take a nature walk, sort items from nature, classify items from nature, observe natural items, protect God's world, plant, cultivate, reflect on or relate to creation and the Creator.

Create Engaging Online Studies

Leading a virtual group has unique challenges. The 2020 pandemic proved that groups can survive and, in many ways, thrive in an online environment. Reports from around the country demonstrated that a high percentage of groups reached new people through online meeting tools. To prepare and lead engaging virtual studies, do not forget some cardinal rules:

1. Plan for a shorter teaching session than in a classroom setting. The online teaching experience is different from the classroom. It may seem counterintuitive, but when you are online, less is more. Craft a twenty- to twenty-five-minute Bible study experience, and use the remaining time to allow people to connect relationally.

2. Use "share screen" to introduce images and other content that enhance the study. While people will enjoy seeing one another's faces, they also enjoy seeing interesting images, maps, charts, a Scripture verse, a question, or other things you might share.

3. Get the most out of your group's personal study guide. Just because your Bible study takes place online does not mean you should not use the personal study guide. Use it as you would in an in-person study. Help group members focus on an image, a question, a quote, or the printed Scripture. The personal study guide is a great visual aid in an online environment.

4. Call on people to read and answer questions. Fully engage your group members by asking them to read portions of Scripture or sections of the personal study guide.

5. Do not ask a question and then answer it yourself. Ask group members to respond, even if it takes ten to twenty seconds for them to formulate a response. If you answer your own question, you will train group members to wait for you. Answer your own questions, and group members will never speak up!

6. Ask everyone to mute their microphones if they are not speaking. Many of us spend lots of time at home these days. Muting microphones will reduce background noise and distractions. I have been in online studies during which children ran into one of the group member's rooms, or a dog decided to bark at the mailman. I was even in a meeting in which two squealing piglets made an unexpected appearance!

7. Use PowerPoint tools to maximize engagement. If you lead an online group using a PowerPoint slideshow, several tools are available to you. The software has built-in features like a laser pointer and a highlighter so you can call attention to words and images on the screen. These two features help increase engagement.

8. If you use the "share screen" feature to ask a question, revert to "gallery view" to get people talking. People will respond to a question when they can see their fellow group members. Leaving an image on the screen will reduce people's desire to offer a response to a question.

Let's add the second diagnostic question to our new scorecard for groups. How would you rate your group's Bible study? Are people engaged? Do they respond when questions are asked? Are they contributing to the study?

NEW SCORECARD FOR GROUPS				
		GRADE		
	LEARN AND OBEY GOD'S WORD	A	B	C	D
1	Are group members growing as disciples?				
2	Are Bible studies well prepared and engaging?				
3					
4					

Main Ideas

1. Preparation is an important part of creating engaging Bible studies. Last-minute preparation never leads to quality Bible studies.

2. There is more than one way to communicate biblical truths to people. Research has demonstrated there are eight learning approaches, and people prefer to learn in different ways. Variety is important in creating engaging studies that people want to attend.

3. The group leader does not have to do all the talking. In fact, it is best if group members talk just as much as the group leader does.

Questions for Discussion

1. To give yourself more preparation time throughout the week, how might you budget time each day to prepare for your upcoming Bible study?

2. Review "Prepare the Meeting Space" section of the chapter and ask yourself how you could arrange your Bible study space so that discussion and interactions are maximized.

3. In what ways would your Bible study group benefit if you were to incorporate the eight learning approaches in your teaching? What are the top two ways you prefer to learn? How do you see those evidenced in the way you guide your group's Bible study?

To-Do List

1. Evaluate your teaching over the past six weeks. How many of the eight learning approaches have you incorporated?

2. Try preparing your next Bible study by using the daily preparation schedule in this chapter. Once you've led the study, evaluate how preparing daily helped your confidence, your delivery, and your overall experience in leading a Bible study.

3. Commit to use two of the eight learning approaches that are not your favorite ways to learn, understanding that those two ways will resonate with people in your group. Incorporate those into your next Bible study and evaluate how your group responded to those approaches.

Chapter 3

Are Apprentice Leaders
Identified and Developed?

A pprenticeship has a long history, dating all the way back
to early Egypt and Babylon. Apprentices were developed so that skills could be passed down from one craftsman
to another, ensuring that there were always enough artisans
to serve the needs of society. The Code of Hammurabi
of Babylon, which dates from the eighteenth century BC,
required artisans to teach their crafts to the next generation.
In Rome and other ancient societies, many craftsmen were
slaves, but in the later years of the Roman Empire, craftsmen
began to organize into independent colleges to uphold the
standards of their trades.[2]

Craft guilds emerged in the thirteenth century AD. An
apprentice would serve for several years under the supervision
of a master craftsman. These master craftsmen controlled
all aspects of the trade. They managed everything from the
quality of products produced, to working conditions, to how
goods were produced. As an alternative to college, technical
and vocational schools emerged in the last century to help
students learn a trade under the supervision of masters of a
particular kind of work.

History has its share of famous people who began as humble apprentices. Elvis Presley apprenticed as an electrician. Music was something he did on the side while he learned his trade. Leonardo da Vinci started his career as an apprentice painter. He went on to create such works as *The Last Supper* and the *Mona Lisa*. And then there is Henry Ford, who apprenticed as a machinist after leaving the family farm in 1879. My father earned his real estate broker's license and opened a small real estate firm. After graduating from college with a degree in business administration and a minor in finance and real estate, I apprenticed with him for two years before the Lord called me into full-time ministry.

You, too, have possibly apprenticed with a more highly skilled person for a time.

> When groups have an apprentice in place, they are signaling their seriousness about reproducing their group and launching a new one.

As we create the new scorecard for groups, group leaders must ask themselves the hard question, "Is our group developing apprentice leaders?" If God's people are going to learn and live God's Word, they will need new leaders and new groups.

While many groups may have a substitute teacher, that is not the same as having an apprentice. A substitute teacher is just that—someone to lead one-off sessions when the group's leader cannot be present. A substitute's job is done when the session is over. On the other hand, an apprentice is intentionally recruited and prepared either to leave the group and start a new one or to step into the group's primary teaching role when the current leader steps down. Succession planning begins when a group leader selects a person in the group to become the apprentice. When groups have an apprentice in place, they are signaling their seriousness about reproducing their group and launching a new one.

Apprenticeship in the Bible

If apprenticeship means learning the skills and knowledge needed to perform a specific task, there are examples of this in the Bible. Moses and Joshua, Elijah and Elisha, Jesus and His disciples, and Paul and Timothy are just a few of the apprentice relationships that can be observed.

Apprenticing involved the accumulation of knowledge, experience, and wisdom from the master. It also involved a relationship between two people, with one preparing the other to have an effective ministry. Paul said to Timothy, "But you have followed my teaching, conduct, purpose, faith, patience, love, and endurance, along with the persecutions and sufferings that came to me in Antioch, Iconium, and Lystra. . . . But as for you, continue in what you have learned and firmly believed. You know those who taught you" (2 Tim. 3:10–11, 14).

The story of Moses and Joshua is especially intriguing. God did not allow Moses to lead the Israelites into the promised land. God allowed Moses to see the land, but not to enter it. Instead, God chose his successor, Joshua, to lead the people into their new homeland. This story contains several insights that may serve group leaders today as they prepare to raise up new leaders.

1. Moses recognized and accepted the temporary nature of leadership. The Bible records God's words to Moses about the end of his leadership over Israel. Moses pleaded with God, saying, "'Please let me cross over and see the beautiful land on the other side of the Jordan, that good hill country and Lebanon.' But the LORD . . . said to me, 'That's enough! Do not speak to me again about this matter . . . for you will not cross the Jordan'" (Duet. 3:25–27). Today leaders must embrace the reality that their present leadership roles are temporary. We do what all leaders have done throughout time: we lead for a season; then someone succeeds us. If you lead a group, never think of it as "your group." The reality is that the people you lead are not yours. They belong to your heavenly Father. You and I are temporary stewards, shepherds who watch over the Master's sheep. We are accountable to Him for their care and well-being. A day will come when you step down from leadership, and the only question that remains will be, "Who will replace you and move the group forward?" Moses accepted the fact that he would no longer lead the people of God and that Joshua would have the privilege of going forward with them.

> If you lead a group, never think of it as "your group." The reality is that the people you lead are not yours. They belong to your heavenly Father.

2. *God revealed Moses's successor to him.* "But commission Joshua and encourage and strengthen him, for he will cross over ahead of the people and enable them to inherit the land that you will see" (Deut. 3:28). If you look around your Bible study group and do not immediately see a successor, do not lose hope. Ask God to reveal that person to you. Make this a matter of prayer. Look for the person who has the characteristics mentioned in chapter 1.

3. Moses affirmed the new leader to God's people and helped the transition process. In Numbers 27:22–23, Moses ensured a smooth succession by placing his hands on Joshua in front of the priest, Eleazar, and all the people. There could be no mistaking that God led Moses to identify Joshua as his successor. The two worked together for years in leading God's people. When it is time for a group leader to pass the baton of leadership to another person, may that person have the heart of Moses to do the right thing and affirm the new leader. Change is difficult, but if the transition is managed well, people tend to accept the new normal with a sense of hope and optimism.

Every Ongoing Group Needs an Apprentice

In his book *Missionary Sunday School*, David Francis made the case for groups to have apprentice leaders. He said that by having an apprentice, the group signaled its intent to be missional. An apprentice, he said, was the number one indicator that a group is serious about reaching new people for Christ. An apprentice leader meant that the group would likely expand by starting a new group. The group might send out the apprentice to start that group, or the current leader might leave the group to do that while the apprentice remained behind to lead the original group. Either way, starting a new group to reach new people was top of mind.

> Without an apprentice, there is no succession plan.

Without an apprentice, there is no succession plan. In churches across the country group leaders suddenly announce their plan to leave, step down, or take a sabbatical.

Unfortunately, many groups are left without an apprentice waiting in the wings to lead the group. No one steps up to lead because an apprentice has not been groomed to serve.

We have not because we ask not. Groups do not have apprentice leaders because an apprentice has not been identified or recruited and intentionally prepared to lead. To change the status quo in groups, group leaders must become intentional in selecting, recruiting, and encouraging apprentice leaders to serve. It has been said that insanity is doing the same things you have been doing but expecting different results. To make certain our churches are positioned to grow and reach new people, we need new groups with new leaders. Apprentice leaders are vital in that process.

During my seminary days, I worked a part-time job in the evenings selling men's clothing on commission for a national retailer. I learned a lot about the retail business. I was trained to talk about the features of a product but to stress the benefits. "Benefits sell the product," I was told. I was also told another valuable piece of advice: ask for the sale! It is one thing to talk about a product and its features and benefits, but at some point in the conversation, any good salesman must ask, "Would you like to put this on your credit card, or do you want to pay cash?" I had to call the customer to action.

It is one thing to talk about recruiting an apprentice, but at some point you have to "ask for the sale" and call for a decision. Group leaders must ask for the sale! It is up to each group leader to select an apprentice and invite him to become a leader in training.

Selecting an Apprentice

The time for selecting an apprentice is now. The starting point is your group. Look around at your group members and ask yourself, *Who has the potential to teach and guide this group or to start a new one soon? Who will the people follow?* Review the qualities of leaders from the first chapter. Look for a person who possesses those traits.

After you have prayed and heard from God, approach your potential apprentice. Set an appointment and invite the person into an apprentice relationship. Establish a duration for the training to take place. (I will share a six-month plan shortly.) Communicate your expectations, such as "I expect sometime after the end of the apprenticeship that you will lead this group (or a new group)." Answer the potential leader's questions, pray, and set a time for him to give his answer.

Once the new apprentice has accepted the opportunity to join you in leadership, make this known to your group. Much like Moses blessed Joshua in the sight of the people, bless the apprentice leader in a formal way. Pray for this person with the group, asking God to use the apprentice to launch a new group or to lead the current one.

Five Steps for Developing an Apprentice

Once you have done the initial work of selecting an apprentice, you must develop that person into a new group leader. Where do you start? What do you do? Don't worry. It is not as complicated as you might think. Years ago I learned from a Christian leader, a former businessman, who began using his experience and expertise to help pastors become more effective leaders. This man wrote a series of books, and in one of them he outlined a five-step plan for developing future leaders.[3] I have found these steps helpful, and I hope you will, as well. Other leaders have written about them, too, and if you search online under the topic of apprenticeship or apprenticing, these basic steps will appear in this form or another:

Step One: The leader models and the apprentice watches. This foundational step in developing a new leader depends upon the apprentice watching and learning from the leader. When the apprentice and the leader spend time together, the apprentice asks questions about his or her observations, and the catalytic process begins.

Step Two: The leader models and the apprentice assists. As the relationship deepens, the leader continues to model the behaviors and skills the apprentice must develop. During this stage, the leader assigns certain tasks to the apprentice. Assisting with the primary leadership tasks builds confidence in the apprentice which leads to the next phase of the person's development.

Step Three: The apprentice leads and the leader assists. By this time, the apprentice has observed the leader. They have had many conversations and debriefings, and the apprentice begins to lead by exhibiting the behaviors and skills of the leader. The leader assists the apprentice if needed but resists rushing in to "save the day." Giving assistance requires the leader to be positive and affirming and to gently correct the apprentice if needed. The goal is to nurture the emerging leader, not to crush him.

Step Four: The apprentice leads and the leader watches. The apprentice's skills continue to grow to the point that he has confidence in his ability to lead well. The apprentice knows that the leader is there for him if needed, but the apprentice now knows what must be done, and he does it. The leader's presence is a comfort, and knowing he is available boosts the confidence level of the apprentice even further, but the leader only steps in if requested by the apprentice. The apprentice is very close to "going solo."

Step Five: The apprentice leads and a new person observes. Mission accomplished! The apprentice has now replicated the work of the leader. The leader's modeling of the work, plus his presence during the mentorship process, has allowed him to replicate himself in another person. The leader moves on to recruit and train a new apprentice, while the apprentice (now a new leader) finds someone to train as well. The leader who recruited the apprentice now moves on to develop another person. The new leader, the former apprentice, invites a potential leader to watch and observe him. This keeps the process of leader development moving forward in the organization.

Now that we have a simple framework for training an apprentice, let's envision what this might look like in the development of an apprentice for an adult Bible study group.

A Six-Month Plan for Developing an Apprentice

Following the five steps for developing an apprentice leader, let's create a realistic six-month plan for that process. If your church decides to get serious about developing apprentices, you will consistently create a new pipeline of available group leaders twice a year. A steady supply of new leaders will revolutionize most churches. Imagine how it could change your church if you had new leaders waiting to begin a teaching ministry.

Months 1 and 2: After identifying and recruiting an apprentice, the group leader should allow the apprentice to observe how the leader teaches the group. During this time, the apprentice identifies how the group leader starts and ends the Bible studies and how the group leader engages people to study the Bible. The apprentice should be given his own set of teaching materials equal to what the group leader has. He should also follow the teaching plan as the group leader teaches to see what he adds or omits. In between Bible study sessions, the apprentice and the group leader should meet to allow the apprentice an opportunity to ask questions and be coached further.

Month 3: After eight weeks of observation, the apprentice should begin to lead a portion of the Bible study each week. The apprentice can open the study by leading the group to pray. He could introduce the topic of the Bible study in a creative and engaging way, and he could transition the members into the Bible study. At this time, the apprentice should support the group leader by leading and teaching about a third of the lesson. The role of the apprentice is to assist the group leader. During this time, the apprentice will have opportunities to gain confidence.

Month 4. By this time, the apprentice should take more ownership of the entire Bible study time, teaching at least half of the study with the group leader. He could be assigned any combination of beginning the group time, teaching the Bible study, and closing the session. The leader who recruited him is there to observe and offer constructive feedback after each lesson.

Month 5: At the start of the fifth month, the process of developing the apprentice is in full swing. The apprentice continues to lead in significant ways while the group leader watches and observes him. The group leader only steps in if absolutely needed. The apprentice continues an ongoing coaching relationship with the leader during these last two months, helping him sharpen his teaching and leadership skills.

Month 6: The apprentice now completes the training period in these final four weeks. The apprentice has gained experience and confidence and is able either to lead the current group (if that has been the goal) or to start a new group and lead it himself. Both the apprentice and the leader will ultimately select two new potential group leaders and mentor them as well. The cycle continues to repeat itself, and the church will have an abundance of workers in time. If this model is followed, one group could produce two new leaders each year. Just think how that would benefit your church's teaching ministry if adult groups started new ones or sent out workers to lead preschool, kids, student, and adult groups. It would be a game changer in churches.

Six Things Every Apprentice Needs

During my short real estate career after graduating from college, I became my father's apprentice. He taught me the ins and outs of writing contracts, negotiating deals, showing houses, and relating to buyers and sellers. When I was called into ministry and began my first full-time staff position, the pastor apprenticed me in how to write sermons, make hospital visits, and lead meetings. We spent a lot of time together in those early days. After a season, I went on to lead my own staff of team members.

Apprenticing someone is a rewarding experience, but it requires a few things of the one who is leading the apprentice. The person you apprentice needs six key things during the process to maximize his success.

1. *The apprentice needs access to the person mentoring him.* A productive relationship with an apprentice is one in which the two people have set aside blocks of time to meet regularly. It is not easy to lead someone from a distance. It is even harder if there is no real relationship with the person being apprenticed. Time on the calendar is paramount. When an in-person meeting is not possible, a virtual meeting is the next best thing.

2. *The apprentice needs to know how to develop an engaging Bible study.* A person who has committed to be your apprentice needs to know how you prepare your Bible studies. He also needs to know how to use the various teaching helps your church provides. Whatever teaching resources your church provides to group leaders should also be made available to each group's apprentice leader. Apprentices must become familiar with the tools that help them create engaging Bible studies.

3. *The apprentice needs opportunities.* It is one thing to be an apprentice. It is completely different to allow that person to have

opportunities to lead the group. In addition to training the apprentice in the art of teaching the group, the group leader should provide opportunities for the apprentice to visit and pray for group members who are in the hospital. There should also be opportunities for the apprentice to reach out to absentee group members. It is even a good idea to allow the apprentice to interact with potential group members, following up with them whenever they visit the group's Bible study.

4. *The apprentice needs feedback.* People thrive on feedback. Whether or not they want it, they need it. People often wonder if they are doing the right things. Giving feedback is not always easy. There are times when an apprentice needs to hear that he has messed up and how to go about making improvements. He may need some "course correction" from his leader. I heard someone say that the key to this is to step on someone's shoes without messing up their shine. That is more art than science!

5. *The apprentice needs encouragement.* There are times an apprentice needs to hear, "You nailed it! Great job!" They need to hear that you believe in them and that you see the progress they are making. Praise is oxygen to a person's soul. We all need it! Do not be disingenuous when you share positive comments with the apprentice.

6. *The apprentice needs public support and affirmation.* Occasionally, it is appropriate to brag on the apprentice in front of others. "I really

thought you brought out some great points during that Bible study," or "I can see that you are ready to lead your own group!" are great things to say to an apprentice. These kinds of statements instill confidence and affirm the apprentice's good work and are even more valuable if they are made in the presence of others.

For centuries the practice of training apprentices has existed. In society apprentices become master craftsmen and repeat the process, ensuring that there are workers who meet people's needs. The church needs apprentices, too. We must ensure that future generations have skilled, able, and equipped leaders who will carry out the Great Commission, teaching people to obey all that Jesus taught.

The new scorecard for groups is continuing to grow. By recruiting apprentice leaders, we position group members to learn and live God's Word. Adult groups expand by starting new ones, and apprentice leaders can be encouraged to lead groups in student and kids' ministries. Apprentice leaders help the church learn and live God's Word in all age groups.

Here is what our new scorecard looks like at this point. Remember, we are moving away from evaluating groups solely on attendance. Rate your Bible study group below. What grade would you give in the important task of identifying and developing apprentice leaders?

NEW SCORECARD FOR GROUPS				
		GRADE		
LEARN AND OBEY GOD'S WORD	A	B	C	D
1	Are group members growing as disciples?				
2	Are Bible studies well prepared and engaging?				
3	Are apprentice leaders identified and developed?				
4					

Main Ideas

1. Groups need apprentice leaders to have future leaders for the group as well as new leaders the group can send out to serve in other ministries of the church.

2. Apprentice leaders should be trained using a six-month process. The process allows them to observe, to practice leading with the group leader, and to lead by themselves as the group leader observes and makes suggestions as needed.

3. If apprentice leaders are not identified and developed, groups will not have future leaders, nor will the church have enough new leaders to grow its various ministries.

Questions for Discussion

1. Who in your Bible study group has the potential to become an apprentice leader? List their names in the margin.

2. What qualities does that person(s) possess that would make them a candidate for becoming an apprentice? What about them caught your eye?

3. Are you comfortable as a group leader with the idea of training your successor? How do you feel about training and releasing some of your group's best leaders?

To-Do List

1. Pray for the potential group leaders who are in your Bible study group today. Which one(s) does God want you to apprentice so they are prepared to lead?

2. If you are not currently a group leader, is there a reason you could not become an apprentice to your group's leader? Ask to be apprenticed by reaching out to your group's leader and offer to be apprenticed for six months.

3. Look back at the list of things apprentice leaders need. In the space below, rank them in order from easiest to hardest for you to deliver. Being aware of the ones that are hardest for you will help you compensate so that your apprentice is well served.

Chapter 4

Are New Groups
Started Regularly?

It was November 1992, and I was getting ready to start my final semester of seminary in January. November was also the month that I was called by a small mission church to become its first discipleship pastor. There were forty-four people in Bible study on launch Sunday, and two teachers quit after teaching their first lessons that day.

Honestly, I did not think I would be at this fledgling church for very long. I remember telling my wife, "Pack your bags and say goodbye to your mom." I thoroughly expected to finish my final semester of school and move on. At least that was my plan.

At the end of May 1993, I walked across the stage as a graduate of Southwestern Baptist Theological Seminary. My wife, parents, sister, and grandparents were in attendance. I was still on staff at that small mission church. Tammy and I did not feel God calling us away to a new place of ministry, so we committed to wait until we heard His voice clearly. In the meantime, we continued to serve the little mission church's congregation.

God chose to leave us at that mission church for more than ten years! I am so glad He did because this is where I learned how to "do groups." The Sunday school ministry grew from forty-four members to more than twenty-four hundred members during that decade.

Let's go back to November 1992.

The church had one building that included a worship center that sat just over a hundred people. The church building had one hallway with six classrooms. So, how did that church become an award-winning Sunday school with only those spaces and a handful of Bible study groups? Well, it didn't. It grew when it provided new groups and new space for Bible study.

Through the financial generosity of one of the church's families, a man and his wife gifted the church $40,000 to buy its first portable building, and on the day we opened it as additional Sunday school space, attendance increased by one hundred people. One hundred people in one day! The pastor and I looked at each other and asked, "I wonder what would happen if we did that again?"

We asked this generous family for their financial help once more since the first portable provided the much-needed space for starting new Sunday school groups. He and his wife saw that new groups helped the church reach new people, and the family eagerly agreed to give another $40,000 for a second portable building. I am so grateful that God places people with the spiritual gift of giving in our churches.

We ordered a second building, and, sure enough, it happened again.

Months later, that second portable was delivered, and the church started new Bible study groups in it as well. On the Sunday we opened the second building, the total attendance in Sunday school grew by another hundred people! Two buildings—two hundred people.

We discovered a foundational truth about groups ministry: *if you want to reach more people, you need more groups.* To have more groups, you need more space! It is an old concept, but it is highly effective.

Over my ten years at this church, we continued to buy portable buildings, and every time we did, we grew by a hundred people. We put large letters on the exterior of the buildings, and today they are still standing and being used! My son Josh and his wife, Amanda, live in a neighborhood just under a mile from this church. Every time we go home to Texas to visit them, I drive through the parking lot of this church where I served as the church's first discipleship pastor. I remember the great things I saw God do there as we reached new people for Christ. Today I see those seven portable buildings when I drive by the church's campus. They still have the letters A, B, C, D, E, F, and G on the side of them, and I thank God for providing those for our church. Without them and the dozens of new groups that started, the church would not have grown as it did.

> We discovered a foundational truth about groups ministry: *if you want to reach more people, you need more groups.*

New groups reach new people. Period.

And yes, those seven portables were not enough to provide space for all the people God sent our way, so we built a $2 million education building and started two more hours of Sunday school. I even had to rent a school just up the road. We bussed groups to the school each Sunday. We even asked groups to meet in homes within walking distance of the campus.

New Groups and the New Scorecard

The old scorecard values attendance; the number of people in groups has always been king. Over the years, the church and its groups may have elevated the attendance metric a bit too much. It is possible we have ignored one of the main ways of looking at the health of groups, whether they are starting new ones or not. Healthy groups grow, and then they begin new ones.

A pastor I served with summed it up this way: "Healthy things grow, and growing things change." Groups change by launching new ones. They change because friends we love act in faith and leave the group to help start the new group. In time, new people come to the Bible study group and find a home there, replacing those who left to start the new group. This should be the rhythm of all healthy, kingdom-focused groups. Healthy groups grow. They release people and start new groups. New people are reached, and the process continues.

> New groups reach new people. Period!

I was recently asked to help evaluate a church's teaching ministry that was in decline. I was provided with a notebook that contained ten years of attendance records. After quickly reviewing the church's attendance data that spanned a decade, I laid the notebook aside, called the pastor, and asked this question: "When was the last time you started a new group?"

Silence.

The pastor said he would check with another staff member and get back to me. Within a few hours he called me back with disappointing but expected news. "We haven't started a

new group for as long as any of us can remember," he said.
I told him that I had heard all I needed to hear to properly
diagnose a big problem in the church's Sunday school ministry. The community was growing—you might even say it was
booming—but the church had not started any new groups in
over five years. This church's Sunday school was in decline.
I almost said it was in a period of stagnation, but everyone
knows there is no such thing as stagnation. Bible study
groups are in one of two categories: growing or declining.

Gravity is a principle I do not challenge. I have visited
the Grand Canyon on two occasions. When I peered over the
edge to take some photos, I made sure I stayed behind the
guardrail. If I got too close to the edge, I am confident that
gravity would win, and I would find myself looking up from
the canyon floor. Every year two or three people die when
they fall into the Grand Canyon.[4] I have made sure that I am
not one of them. Gravity is a principle that is ever present.

There are principles that govern new groups as well, and
they are always in effect. I have led the formation of new
groups as a discipleship pastor. I have started two new groups
myself over the last several years and have observed these
principles up close. They are real, and I respect them.

- *New groups will reach ten people on average.*
  Let's say you start a new adult group, and
  it reaches six people. You might say, "Aha,
  it didn't reach ten!" But if you consider that
  those six people have children that are now
  in a group, too, it probably exceeded ten! I
  have started two adult groups recently, and
  both reached more than thirty adults each!
  We averaged anywhere from twelve to sixteen people in attendance on any given week
  in both groups.

- *New groups will grow faster than existing groups.* Groups that have been together longer than eighteen months tend to turn inward. It is understandable. The group members have built relationships, prayed for one another, served together, and become a family. When a new group starts, it is much easier for people who have struggled to connect suddenly to find themselves with a host of new friends. In addition, the longer a group has been together, the harder it is for new people to be assimilated. You feel like an outsider, and people are slow to let you into their inner circle of friends. Not so with a new group!
- *New groups are more outward focused than existing groups.* New groups tend to be more excited about having potential new group members in their midst. They tend to invite friends to the new group and are sensitive to make guests feel welcome.

How many new groups should you start in a year? The answer is, "It depends." It depends on some key factors such as:

- *What is your church's annual growth goal next year?* If you want to grow by thirty people, the simple math says you would want to start three new groups.
- *What is your church's percentage of churn?* Churn is defined as the number of people who leave your church each year. Churches tend to have 10–20 percent annual churn;

it depends on the church. Every church will have people who move away, die, or break ties for one reason or another. If your church loses 10 percent of its members each year, and you have a church of two hundred people, you now need to start two groups just to cover your churn because about twenty people will leave for whatever reason. If you add the growth goal of starting three groups to the need to start two more groups to cover churn, you need to start five groups this year.

- *What will your space and schedule allow?* It is one thing to want to grow by adding groups, but do you have the physical space to do that? If you start three new groups for preschoolers, do you have the space to start a new group or two for the parents of those children? If you want to add groups for teenagers, do you have room for them, or would you need to add a second hour of Bible study to allow for growth?

- *What is your church's attitude toward starting new groups?* I have known churches whose members were resistant to adding new groups. I have also known churches, like the mission church I was a part of for ten years, that would do just about anything to grow and add new groups to reach people, kind of like the people of Nehemiah's day. Nehemiah 4:6 records a momentous occasion: "We rebuilt the wall until the entire wall was joined together up to half its height, for the people had the will to keep working." It is amazing what you can accomplish when people want to roll up their sleeves and get to work. Preaching about reaching new people, sharing vision for growth, and praying for God to give the church ways to minister to people keep the need for new groups fresh on the minds of church members. The adage is true: "If it is important to the pastor, it becomes important to the church." If you are a pastor, leverage your influence to help start new groups.

- *Is your community growing?* I understand that not every church is in a city or town that is growing. Many rural churches are in areas where decline has or is taking place. Should those churches start new groups? The answer is yes. Even though a region may be in decline, there are always plenty of unchurched and unreached people in the region, city, or county. For those churches, perhaps the new groups are not started at the church. Instead, a more missionary mindset would say to start new groups in off-campus locations like apartment complexes, schools, or offices. A neighborhood Bible study might be just the thing to attract new people to a study close to them. If your church is in a more rural location, look for other places from which to launch new groups. This does not have to be done at the church!

New Groups Need Trained Leaders

In the previous chapter I mentioned the need for apprentice leaders to be trained and released into service.

Apprenticing is one of two foundational ways group leaders must be trained. Apprenticing new leaders is a strategic way to onboard them, but that training only lasts for a limited time. Once they begin their teaching ministry, they will require a new kind of training: *ongoing* training.

Ongoing training takes place through strategy. Research has demonstrated that churches with a regular cadence of training grow more than churches that do not have a plan. A survey of more than twenty-five hundred churches in Georgia determined that if a church did not have training for its leaders, the teaching ministries declined by -2.1 percent in the time period examined. However, if churches had quarterly or monthly training, they grew between 13 and 14 percent during the same four-year period.[5]

Training requires a church to budget for it. It must also give it priority time on the church calendar. No other meetings should conflict with it. Group leaders should also be enlisted with the expectation that they will take part in the ongoing training offered by the church. A note to pastors: make certain you provide training for your group leaders. You do not have to lead the training yourself, pastor, but you must see that someone is assigned this most important task. And for the group leaders who are reading this book, go to the training offered by your church! Training makes a difference.

Celebrate New Groups

My granddaughter Nora Gail Braddy was born in February 2021. She is the first girl born into our family in almost thirty years. My wife and I purchased plane tickets and flew to see her just after she was born. We prayed for her, took gifts to her, and celebrated her arrival with my son and his wife. Births are a big deal!

New Bible study groups should be celebrated as well. Something new has been birthed. The church is experiencing new life and health, new leaders have accepted God's call to lead, and we should not let opportunities go by to remind our fellow church members that new groups are blessings from God. The church family can be introduced to the new group leader, the new group members who birth the group, and the congregation can learn who the new group is designed to reach—young adults, single moms, senior adults, or others. With that knowledge, the entire church can celebrate and support it.

Start New Groups at Strategic Times

There are some occasions when starting a new group (or groups) makes the most sense. While you can start a new group any time you have a trained leader and the space for it, you will have a better chance of helping the new group launch well if you start it at one of these times.

1. When a group has been together for eighteen months or more. It is hard for guests to assimilate into groups that have been together longer than eighteen months. When a group approaches its second birthday, it is time to think "start a new group."

2. When an apprentice is ready to start a group. As we have already discussed, you cannot start new groups without new group leaders. When an apprentice is ready, allow him to launch a new Bible study group. I almost said no to someone who was ready to start a group at the beginning of summer. I reasoned that we should wait a few months until vacations were over and people came back to church (attendance at that church dropped quite a bit during the summer). This persistent apprentice convinced me to let him start a group for young couples, and the group took off like a rocket. In summer!

3. When a group fills their meeting space to more than 80 percent of capacity. The 80/20 rule is real. When a group exceeds 80 percent of its seating capacity, the room is visually full. A group can certainly exceed 80 percent of its seating capacity (it is fun to have a full room with no empty seats), but any group that exceeds 80 percent of its seating capacity for very long will almost always drop to an attendance level less than the 80 percent it once exceeded. People need elbow room; adults require fifteen square feet of space each.

4. When the age span of group members is more than ten years. Although a multigenerational group sometimes forms, it is not optimal. The homogeneity principle states that people who are similar in age should be placed together in groups. That means that the maximum age range in any group should not be more than ten years. If it is, it is time to start another group or groups. The homogeneity principle creates better group dynamics and the establishment of relationships between people who have common interests and life experiences.

5. When there are natural times people return to church. Most churches experience a rise in Bible study attendance each fall. It normally begins in August when vacations end and kids go back to school. Starting groups at the first of the year is also wise because people tend to recommit themselves to attending groups. Mid-spring around Easter (or post-Easter to reach the many worshippers who come to church for Easter services) is also a natural time to consider launching new groups.

6. When you realize that a certain people group is underserved. If you look at the kinds of groups your church offers and do not see a group for a particular people group, it is a good time to start one. Arthur Flake, the father of the modern Sunday school movement, listed this as the first of the five steps in his famous formula for building a strong groups ministry. He insisted that the first step is to "know your possibilities." Part of knowing your possibilities for reaching people is knowing who is underserved in the church or in the community. Knowing your possibilities for reaching new people for Christ requires you to look internally *and* externally discover underserved and underreached people.

We are now at the end of the first section of the book, Learn and Obey God's Word. It is the first goal of every Bible study group. It is the *L* in the LIFE acrostic.

We have asked three questions so far in the quest to create a new scorecard for groups. Let's add the fourth question related to starting new groups. Evaluate your group and give it a grade below. Does your group start new ones regularly?

NEW SCORECARD FOR GROUPS		GRADE			
	LEARN AND LIVE GOD'S WORD	**A**	**B**	**C**	**D**
1	Are group members growing as disciples?				
2	Are Bible studies well prepared and engaging?				
3	Are apprentice leaders identified and developed?				
4	**Are new groups started regularly?**				

Main Ideas

1. New groups are necessary to reach new people. Each new group your church starts will reach ten new people on average.

2. New groups need new group leaders, and new group leaders need ongoing training.

3. There are optimal times to start new groups, such as at the beginning of the year or at back-to-school time in the fall.

Questions for Discussion

1. Over the last five years, how many groups have been started because of the actions of your Bible study group? How many do you foresee starting in the next two years?

2. If a member of your group said, "I don't see why we need to start another group. I like ours just the way it is," how would you respond?

3. What underserved people groups can you identify in your church or community that would benefit from having a group to attend that does not exist now?

To-Do Items

1. Talk with your Bible study group about starting a new one. Help them process their thoughts and feelings about this.

2. Consider how your group might go about starting a new one. Would you divide the group in half, ask for volunteers,

or pre-enlist some of your group members to leave with the new group leader?

3. Consider your philosophy about starting new groups. Evaluate if you've had a mindset that has kept your from releasing people because you enjoy teaching a large group. Would you adopt a new mindset that says, "Bible study groups are not a storehouse but a clearinghouse of leaders"?

Measurement 2

Invite People to Become Disciples

Chapter 5

Are Prayers Focused on the Lost?

King Asa is one of my favorite individuals of the Old Testament. His story shows the power of prayer. I love the way his story begins in 2 Chronicles 14.

> Asa did what was good and right in the sight of the LORD his God. He removed the pagan altars and the high places. He shattered their sacred pillars and chopped down their Asherah poles. He told the people of Judah to seek the LORD God of their ancestors and to carry out the instruction and the commands. He also removed the high places and the shrines from all the cities of Judah, and the kingdom experienced peace under him. (vv. 2–5)

Asa was a young king, but he recognized what needed to be done throughout the land. The people of God had strayed from Him. They needed to be challenged to return to God, and Asa determined to start by destroying the false idols erected by God's people. Pagan places and objects of worship were also obliterated. Things went well for Asa and the people. God honored His faithful servant-king.

Then came a true threat to their survival. A million-man army marched northward out of Egypt, and the odds of the two southern tribes surviving the invasion were miniscule. Outnumbered severely and outclassed in weaponry, King Asa and his people faced captivity or death.

And then he prayed.

> Then Asa cried out to the LORD his God, "Lord, there is no one besides you to help the mighty and those without strength. Help us, LORD our God, for we depend on you, and in your name we have come against this large army. LORD, you are our God. Do not let a mere mortal hinder you."
>
> So the LORD routed the Cushites before Asa and before Judah, and the Cushites fled. Then Asa and the people who were with him pursued them as far as Gerar. The Cushites fell until they had no survivors, for they were crushed before the LORD and his army. (vv. 11–13)

Don't you just love it when God shows up? On the day of that battle, God's people learned the power of prayer. A young king fell to his knees and cried out to God, and he was heard. Not only was he heard, but his prayer for salvation from an enemy was answered.

The God who answered Asa's prayer, the God who answered Hezekiah's prayer in 2 Kings, and the God who heard Paul and Silas's prayers in an inner jail cell is the same God we pray to today. He still hears. He still answers, and

His power is still mighty to save. And we know He desires for none to perish and for all to repent.

God is powerful, but groups do not always regularly pray for the salvation of people when they come together for Bible study. Instead, groups tend to focus on the needs of the members. This is not necessarily bad. Groups spend a lot of time praying for the physical, mental, and emotional needs of the members but may not cry out to God to save lost friends or family members.

Somehow we forget to pray for the salvation of people when our Bible study groups come together. God's power is on display on every page of the Bible. His infinite wisdom and power can be seen throughout the created order. We know He is deeply concerned about the eternal destiny of people, so much that He sacrificed Jesus to make a way to eternal life possible. God is powerful, and He is mighty to save, yet prayers for the lost are not always on our lips.

Prayer Is the Starting Point

For Bible study groups to adopt a new scorecard, one of the primary elements that must be measured is whether the group has made praying for the lost a priority. When Jesus gave the church what we know as the Great Commission, He made clear that we are to make disciples. Disciples are made when they accept God's forgiveness through Christ's atoning work on the cross. The starting point for making disciples is the prayers of God's people, and by that I mean praying for specific people by name. We take their names to our heavenly Father, asking Him to do a work in their lives, convict them of sin, and lead them to the point of repentance.

We must pray for specific people. We all know at least one person, probably more, who is living in rebellion against God. The Lord may have already placed that person's name in your mind as you are reading this. There are men, women, boys, and girls who are a heartbeat away from an eternity without God. How can we not lift them up in prayer to the One who died so that they might have eternal life through Him? *We must pray for the Holy Spirit to convict them of their need for Jesus.* I have spoken to multiple people over the years about their need for Jesus. When I worked in student ministry, I took a group of teenagers to Crested Butte, Colorado, for a few days of skiing over spring break. I woke up in the middle of the night to hear strange voices coming from the condominium's living room. Some of the students in our group had met some slightly older guys on the slopes that day, and the three young men had been invited to come and hang out with members of our student group in my condo. I shared what I believed was a clear and articulate summary of the gospel, telling these boys exactly what they needed to do to be forgiven by God. They refused. They ridiculed some of the things I said and even made some outrageous statements about God. They allowed me to pray for them, and then they left for the night. I realized that all the logic in the world was not going to win them over unless the Holy Spirit brought about conviction in their hearts.

As you pray for people who are far from God, remember to ask the Holy Spirit to bring people to a place where they feel convicted about their sin and their inability to save themselves through works or good deeds.

We must pray for someone to share the gospel with them. Paul addressed the need for a verbal presentation of the gospel. In Romans 10, he wrote:

> For everyone who calls on the name of the Lord will be saved.
> How, then, can they call on him they have not believed in? And how can they

believe without hearing about him? And how can they hear without a preacher? And how can they preach unless they are sent? As it is written: How beautiful are the feet of those who bring good news. But not all obeyed the gospel. For Isaiah says, Lord, who has believed our message? So faith comes from what is heard, and what is heard comes through the message about Christ. (vv. 13–17)

For years my father lived in rebellion against God. We were estranged for nearly a year toward the end of his life. My father was always a good provider for our family, but he was emotionally, relationally, and spiritually distant.

As a result of diabetes, he had a series of amputation surgeries in his mid-seventies, losing both of his legs. I was there for both surgeries, but I remember there was something different about the second one. I sat in his hospital room a day before his second amputation and felt prompted by God to speak up and share the gospel. That was one of the most difficult things I have ever done. It was made more difficult because my dad had graduated seminary decades before but walked away from his ministry calling, from the church, and lived like an unbeliever for many years. His choices in life profoundly affected our family in many negative ways.

Over the years I prayed that someone would share the gospel with him because I was not convinced he knew the Lord. As I prayed for my dad to turn back to the Lord, I realized that I was the answer to my own prayer. God revealed that it was my responsibility to share the gospel with him before his second surgery. I did, but he did not respond with a contrite and broken heart. I asked him if he knew for sure that he would go to heaven if he died during the surgery. He responded by saying, "Who knows what happens when you die." I could not believe my ears.

Dad died several weeks after that surgery on a Monday morning in December 2008. I will have to wait until I get to heaven to know if he might have lain in his bed one day after the surgery, thought about my words, remembered what he knew about the gospel, and asked God to forgive him. I hope he did. I would love to see my dad again.

I share all of that to say, as you pray for the salvation of a friend or family member, perhaps even an acquaintance, *you* may be the person God wants to use to share a witness with that person. Be open to that possibility. Which brings me to my last point.

We must pray for our eyes to be opened to see the opportunities around us for sharing the gospel. I will address this more in another chapter, but for now let's just say that we all live in "target-rich environments," to borrow a military metaphor.

Pray with a Sense of Urgency

The third chapter of 2 Peter is one of my favorite chapters in the New Testament. In this section of his epistle, Peter was in the process of responding to an argument directed at him by "scoffers." They doubted that Jesus was going to return bodily to the earth. His critics launched an all-out attack on the gospel by questioning the reality of Jesus's return by asking, "Where is his 'coming' that he promised? Ever since our ancestors fell asleep, all things continue as they have been since the beginning of creation" (2 Pet. 3:4). Under the inspiration of the Holy Spirit, Peter completely dismantled their flawed thinking. He reminded the scoffers that the earth had experienced a cataclysmic event before—the flood! And not only had it experienced the flood, but the creation of the earth was also a cataclysmic event. Peter reminded his opponents that God does not count time like we do, so what feels like a delay to us is not a delay at all from God's perspective. Peter then turned his attention to the future and what will take place. It is a terrifying picture of what awaits the ungodly on the day of the Lord.

Peter wrote that the reason for "delay" in Christ's return is based on God's love for people. Peter spoke of God's patience, not wanting anyone to perish, and for all to come to repentance (2 Pet. 3:9). The day of the Lord will come soon enough, according to Peter. That day will be a worldwide apocalyptic event in which the heavens and earth melt away. The description should motivate all believers to pray urgently for the lost. It will be a dark day for anyone who is not found in Christ upon His return to earth.

Peter concluded this portion of his letter by reminding all believers to "regard the patience of our Lord as salvation" (2 Pet. 3:15). This means that although the scoffers of his day accused God of slackness in returning, that was not what was happening at all. Peter declared that the "delay" of Christ's return is a demonstration of His patience, and every day Jesus does not return is another day for believers to share the gospel with as many people as they can. We must regard the patience of the Lord as salvation, so we pray for people who are living in rebellion to God.

When you think about the future that is waiting for unrepentant people, it changes your prayers for the people in your life who do not know Jesus as Savior. It will change the way your Bible study group prays. Prayers for the group's members will become more balanced over time as they focus more equally on the fate of unbelievers they know, those they meet, and even those in the community they may never meet.

Enlist a Group Prayer Leader

One of the greatest moments in a Bible study group happens when the leader delegates the responsibility for the group's prayer life to one of the members who has a passion for it. A prayer leader helps a group focus on that key aspect of group life. I will take a deeper dive into the responsibilities of prayer leaders in a later chapter.

In a typical group study, the teacher/leader would guide the group's study, allowing the prayer leader to wrap up the group time by leading the members to record prayer requests and pray for them. I have seen groups that pray before the Bible study (which is perfectly fine). The prayer leader would be sensitive to the new scorecard metric of praying for lost persons and would encourage the group to pray for people they know who are not yet believers.

Pray with Regularity and Consistency

Bible study groups can shift the focus of their prayers to be more inclusive of people who are far from God. If your group tends to pray for the needs of its members but not for the salvation of spiritually lost people, you can make changes. If you are a group leader, lead your group to pray for the salvation of people by setting the example and naming people for whom you are praying. Ask your group to add names of people to their prayer lists as well and to the prayer list of the group.

LEVEL	CLASS	COMMUNITY	COMMISSION
Churched	Member	Minister	Missionary
Focus	Me	Us	Them
Unchurched	Conversation	Community	Conversion
Biblical Mandate	Great Confession	Great Commandment	Great Commission
Conversation	What we learned	What they did for me	Where we went
Prayer	General requests	Needs of others	Lost people
Records	Class list	Ministry list	Prospect list
Organization	Teacher, secretary	Fellowship, ministry, prayer, and care-group leaders	Missions leader, outreach leader, apprentices, associates
Biblical Concept	*Kerygma*	*Koinonia*	*Kenosis*

In the book *Connect3*,[6] David Francis described three levels a Bible study group achieves over time. If you look at the Level category and scroll down to the word Prayer, you'll see that David described the kind of prayers you will hear in groups that are at the Class, Community, and Commission stages. In the early stages of a group, prayers are focused on general requests—nothing too serious. As the group grows closer together, however, it reaches the Community level where members demonstrate more vulnerability. Prayer requests focus on the needs of the group members. As the group continues to grow together, a final stage is reached—the Commission level. This is when group members take responsibility for accomplishing the Great Commission. They begin to make disciples by praying for specific people who do not know the Lord. As described in the chart, group members' prayers are focused on lost people. May all our Bible study groups achieve this wonderful stage of group life!

Overcome the Fear of Praying in Public

It is amazing to watch normally conversant group members go silent when prayer time begins. It is a fact of group life that some people are afraid to speak up and are even more fearful of praying out loud. Perhaps they have never done that before or are afraid they won't have the words to say. Maybe they just do not want to trip over their own tongue. The fear of speaking in public is real!

To help your group move beyond the fear of praying publicly, there are a few things you can do. First, do not force anyone to pray. You may accidentally discourage them from attending future group meetings if they do not want to pray out loud. Second, you can subdivide your group members into smaller groups. It is much less intimidating to pray in a group of three than in a group of thirteen. Finally, you can group up people in smaller clusters by gender—men pray with men, women pray with women. This can also reduce the tension that some people feel when asked to pray in front of a larger mixed group.

As we continue to build a new scorecard for Bible study groups, let's add a fifth diagnostic question as we begin a new section of essential work in groups: inviting persons to become disciples. As you consider grading your group on this, be honest! Remember that we want to know as accurately as possible what is taking place in our groups. If you are praying for lost people almost every week, give yourself and your group an A. If you almost never pray for people in that way, honestly evaluate your group and place a check mark elsewhere.

NEW SCORECARD FOR GROUPS				
	GRADE			
INVITE PEOPLE TO BECOME DISCIPLES	A	B	C	D
5	Are prayers focused on the lost?			
6				
7				
8				

Main Ideas

1. In some Bible study groups, prayers tend to be focused on the needs of the group members and not on the eternal destinies of people who do not know Christ as Savior.

2. Group members should be able to articulate their testimonies so others can hear about the difference Jesus has made in their lives.

3. A simple gospel presentation that is memorable and repeatable is needed so that group members are always ready to share Christ with a person who is not yet a believer.

Questions for Discussion

1. How can you encourage your group to pray more regularly for lost persons?

2. As you think about your family, friends, coworkers, and neighbors, which person's salvation will you commit to pray for? List their name(s) below.

3. Do you have assurance of your salvation? If not, who is a trusted Christian friend with whom you can speak about this?

To-Do List

1. Talk with your Bible study group about the importance of adding or reorienting prayers to include people who are not yet believers.

2. Select a simple, memorable, and repeatable gospel presentation and teach it to your group members.

3. Lead your Bible study group members to write their testimonies and practice telling their stories to fellow group members as a way to prepare for a real encounter with someone who does not know Christ.

Chapter 6

Are Group Members Eating with "Sinners and Tax Collectors"?

One of the greatest accusations ever leveled against Jesus was that He spent time with those that religious leaders of His day found to be undesirable or unclean. The way Jesus created margin in His schedule to spend time with sinners is admirable. It also serves as an example for us today.

However, it seems that the longer you and I are in church, we find fewer and fewer people who are not Christians. Most of our friends are from our church. Many of our activities center around church. We must work diligently to spend time with people the way Jesus did. You can see in Jesus's reply to His critics that He was focused intently on one mission: making disciples. He used the encounter below to correct the thinking and theology of the Pharisees who criticized Him.

> Jesus went out again beside the sea. The whole crowd was coming to him, and he was teaching them. Then, passing by, he saw Levi the son of Alphaeus sitting at the tax office, and he said to him, "Follow me," and he got up and followed him.

> While he was reclining at the table in
> Levi's house, many tax collectors and sinners
> were eating with Jesus and his disciples, for
> there were many who were following him.
> When the scribes who were Pharisees saw
> that he was eating with sinners and tax col-
> lectors, they asked his disciples, "Why does
> he eat with tax collectors and sinners?"
> When Jesus heard this, he told them, "It
> is not those who are well who need a doctor,
> but those who are sick. I didn't come to call
> the righteous, but sinners." (Mark 2:13–17)

When we were younger, my wife and I encouraged our two sons to have friends in the "church crowd." In fact, most of their friends were in the student ministries of the two churches where I served on staff. We were well intentioned and rightly motivated, but we could have encouraged them to hang out as much with kids who could be described as "sinners and tax collectors" as we encouraged them to find friends in the church. If I had a mulligan (a golfing term for "do-over"), I would have chosen a different path.

How many of the adults in Bible study groups mainly have Christian friends? I suspect many of them. These churchgoing adults discover they have common beliefs and interests with their fellow group members, and relationships naturally form. Before you know it, most of their friends are from their church and Bible study group. Perhaps only a handful spend time with unchurched people. When group members are invited to pray for the lost and to share Christ with them, they likely find difficulty because they know so few.

Being Comfortable with Being Uncomfortable

Here is the truth: *lost people act like lost people.* Do not expect otherwise, and you will not be disappointed. If you do as Jesus did and follow His example of spending relational time with people who are not believers, you will hear and see some things that will probably make you uncomfortable. Being uncomfortable is part of the process of winning people to Jesus. Spending time with the nonreligious crowd of His day kept Jesus focused on the mission: He came to seek and save the lost. What better place to be than, well, with the lost? If we want to be on mission and influence others for Christ, we must be in proximity to them.

When I was on church staff, Thursdays served as my day off. I liked taking Thursdays off because the price of a round of golf was cheaper on Thursdays than it was on Fridays. I was blessed to live in the center of Dallas-Fort Worth. I had access to multiple golf courses within a twenty-minute drive of my house. I normally spent part of

> If we want to be on mission and influence others for Christ, we must be in proximity to them.

my day playing a round of golf or a few hours working on my chipping and putting.

One Thursday I went to the Bear Creek Golf Course in Grapevine, Texas. I walked into the pro shop and told the attendant that I was a single player who wanted to play a round of golf. He soon paired me with a group of three younger players. I often did this to meet people, play golf, and share the gospel. I soon discovered that these three young men were students at a local college.

I met up with this group on the first tee box. We introduced ourselves, and we teed off. I quickly realized that I was not with a church crowd! They drank beer, used profanity, told coarse jokes, and were generally ill mannered. They were even rude to the young lady who came around with snacks and drinks from time to time, flirting with her and making her uncomfortable.

Did I feel like going home? Yes. But I reminded myself why I was out there playing with strangers. It was my way of spending time with "sinners and tax collectors" since my entire life and work revolved around church. My closest friends were staff members or church members.

And then it happened. It always does. As we stood on the tee box of the fourth hole, one of the guys asked me, "So, Ken, what do you do for a living?" I smiled on the inside because I knew what was about to happen. It had happened several times before in situations like this.

I said, "I have a great job not far from here. I am a pastor at a church just up the road," I said. The guys became instantly aware of their bad behavior. "That's cool," said one of them, breaking the awkward silence. I just kept smiling internally. The second fellow sheepishly said, "Look, we're sorry for the bad language. We didn't know you were a pastor." I assured him that it hadn't offended me and that I was glad to be playing golf with them. They never cursed again during our round! They cleaned up their acts right away. Lost people are going to act like lost people, right?

I kept talking and encouraging them as we played, trying to make a connection. I asked about their backgrounds, school, and work. I asked if they attended a church in the area, and I discovered they did not. At the end of the round as we shook hands on the eighteenth green, I handed each of them one of my business cards with an invitation to play golf again, and I gave them another invitation to visit our Sunday worship service as my guest. I was able to be a witness for Christ, and they discovered that pastors are real people, too. I followed Jesus's example of spending time with sinners and tax collectors.

If you saw me standing next to these men who were drinking one beer after another, you might have been offended. The religious leaders of Jesus's day were certainly offended that He was in proximity to people they deemed undesirable. But if you ever have a thought like that run through your mind, remind yourself that Jesus came to seek and save the lost. The sick need a doctor, not the healthy. Where would Jesus be today if He were here? We might see Him on the golf course, at a sporting event, or at a backyard barbecue hosted by a neighbor. You would find Jesus building relationships with people who need grace and forgiveness. That is where we must be as well. That is the mission. It is an important part of the new scorecard for groups.

Creating Margin

The first step in eating with sinners and tax collectors is the creation of margin in your life. Margin is the time you build into your schedule to make certain you can focus on the things that are most important to you. Margin allows you to slow down so you do not rush past an opportunity to spend time with someone when the opportunity arises.

I have a work calendar with margin built into it. I realized that when I allowed other people to set my schedule and agenda, I found myself being frustrated. I love my weekly schedule because I have blocks of time intentionally scheduled for different aspects of my work and for building relationships with new people.

Think about your calendar.

Look ahead to next week's schedule on your calendar. You may see days of the week that are wide open right now. These can be moments to hang out with sinners and tax collectors. But if you do not calendar the relational time now, something else will crowd it out. You have no margin in your schedule for the sinners and tax collectors you know.

Jesus made time for people in His schedule. He was a busy, sought-after man, but He still created margin. He could have ignored people around Him who wanted His time and attention, but He didn't. Remember the story of the woman who touched His robe in a crowd of people? Luke records this:

> While he was going, the crowds were nearly crushing him. A woman suffering from bleeding for twelve years, who had spent all she had on doctors and yet could not be healed by any, approached from behind and touched the end of his robe. Instantly her bleeding stopped.
>
> "Who touched me?" Jesus asked.
>
> When they all denied it, Peter said, "Master, the crowds are hemming you in and pressing against you."
>
> "Someone did touch me," said Jesus. "I know that power has gone out from me." When the woman saw that she was discovered, she came trembling and fell down before him. In the presence of all the people, she declared the reason she had touched him and how she was instantly healed. "Daughter," he said to her, "your faith has saved you. Go in peace." (Luke 8:42–48)

Jesus could have kept moving along, but He stopped and allowed Himself to be interrupted. Sometimes when you and I gaze at the crowd, we just see a crowd. I believe that when Jesus looked at a crowd, He saw individuals. He saw people who were downtrodden. These kinds of people would move Him to tears as He wept over Jerusalem. Jesus set a tremendous example of what it means to slow down long enough to see individuals.

I am sure you remember the story of Zacchaeus. It is found in Luke 19:1–10 and is another example of Jesus creating margin to spend time with someone who was already an outcast as a tax collector. Zacchaeus climbed a sycamore tree to see Jesus (the crowds were too great for him to get a good spot at the front); he was a small man, after all. Jesus called out to him and told him to come down because He needed to stay at his house that evening. People in the crowd grumbled and said, "He's gone to stay with a sinful man" (Luke 19:7). Yes, He did! That is what Jesus liked to do. He created margin so that He could stop and slow down long enough to relate to people. It changed their lives every time.

Authenticity Wins

Do you know the difference between houses built fifty years ago and those built today? Porches and fences! People once had large front porches with rocking chairs and swings, and at certain times during the day or evening, neighbors would come out, talk with one another, and build authentic relationships. Today we pull into the garage or drive behind an iron gate and go inside for the rest of the day. People used to have fences, but not the tall privacy fences we have today. No, they had shorter fences they could talk over. They had chain-link fences they could see through, and neighbors talked across those fences to get to know one another. People were authentic, had relationships, and made time for one another.

If you become convinced that creating time in your schedule to spend with a person or persons who are not Christians might be a good investment, remember one thing: *people do not want to be treated like projects.*

The quickest way to alienate people is to make them feel like an evangelism project. You'll lose the chance to speak into their life if they feel like another notch on your evangelical belt. Christians who genuinely want to develop a relationship with a nonbeliever know that authenticity is important in this process. The opportunity to share the gospel may not happen suddenly, but consistent relationship building over time, a nonjudgmental attitude, and an openness to hear their stories are so important!

> The quickest way to alienate people is to make them feel like an evangelism project.

I am sure you're like me and can spot a fake a mile away. We should care for people whether they respond to the gospel or not. We must love them regardless of whether they decide to attend a worship service or Bible study group and whether they allow us to share our story of spiritual transformation with them. We must value them because they were created in God's image and need a Savior.

People Don't Drift toward Jesus

Every person needs Jesus, but we do not always seek Him. Scripture says that we are like sheep, and we have all drifted away from the Shepherd; we have gone astray.

Because people drift away from Jesus, Christians must seek those people. We know that the lost are in our neighborhoods, workplaces, families, and communities. By following Christ's example, we can solve the drifting problem one person and one family at a time. It starts when we accept our role in showing them biblical hospitality, spend time with them, and love them unconditionally. When our Bible study groups have a fellowship, the first thing we must ask is, "Whom can I invite who is not a believer? Whom do I know who has walked away from God but needs to be claimed for Christ?"

Jesus spent time with the undesirable. He loved them, honored them, healed them, spoke to them, and related to them. The religious people wrote them off, but not Jesus. He communicated His love for them by spending time with them and by sharing the truth of the gospel with them. He was not afraid to eat with sinners and tax collectors, nor was He afraid of what people might say. The critics talked about Jesus behind His back, and they might talk behind yours and mine, as well.

Jesus had a higher purpose: to do the will of His heavenly Father. His Father's will is for all people to be saved. Jesus related to sinners and tax collectors, spent time with them, and ventured into their space. He met them where they lived and worked. He loved them enough not to be dissuaded by the religious leaders who criticized Him. One of the greatest compliments anyone gave Jesus came from the Pharisees: "He eats with sinners and tax collectors."

Are your group members spending time with sinners and tax collectors? Do you find your group focused on the members, or are they focused on people who need to see that God's people care for them? Optimally, your group and mine will spend time doing both: we should spend time with our brothers and sisters in Christ, but we should also create margin so that we can hang out with people who do not believe or act like we do.

NEW SCORECARD FOR GROUPS					
		GRADE			
	INVITE PEOPLE TO BECOME DISCIPLES	A	B	C	D
5	Are prayers focused on the lost?				
6	Are group members eating with "sinners and tax collectors"?				
7					
8					

Main Ideas

1. Jesus's critics accused Him of spending time with "undesirable people." Jesus used the opportunity to rebuke the Pharisees and explain His true mission: to seek and save the lost.

2. The longer Christians attend church, the fewer non-Christians they know. Intentionally spending time with people who are not believers is important for all Christians so they can build relationships, build bridges, and win the opportunity to talk about Jesus.

3. We must intentionally create margin in our weekly schedules that gives us time to relate to people who are outside the church family.

Questions for Discussion

1. What might you give up each week to create some extra time for relating to people who are not connected to your church, your group, or to God?

2. How might your Bible study group help its members connect to people who are living apart from God?

3. When was the last time you built a relationship for the purpose of sharing the gospel? Jot down some of the key things you remember from that encounter.

To-Do List

1. Pray for God to give you opportunities to influence a friend, family member, coworker, or neighbor for Jesus by building a stronger relationship with them.

2. Perform an act of service for a neighbor who does not attend church. Watch for an open door to share the gospel.

3. Invite non-Christians to your group's fun fellowship events. Use those times to build bridges and establish friendships with the "sinners and tax collectors" known to your group's members.

Chapter 7

Are New Persons Invited to Connect with the Group?

W hen my sons were young, they loved getting mail. If anyone sent them a letter, it was a special day at the Braddy house. Postcards from grandparents were always well received, as were random pieces of mail from dentists and doctors who recognized their birthdays. However, if one of my boys received an invitation to a friend's birthday party, that was extra special. Both of my boys loved receiving those kinds of invitations! An invitation meant they were valued; it meant they were going to be around their friends. They felt included and "part of the club."

**47% joined a group because the leader
or a member of the group invited them**

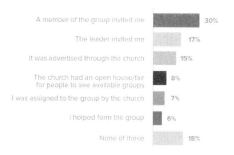

Invitations Are Important

We have known for a long time that invitations to attend Bible study groups are important. I have led weekly Bible study groups over the past few years, and I can count on one hand the number of guests who just showed up to participate with the group. Almost all guests attend because someone in the group asked them to participate in a Bible study or a fellowship event.

Lifeway Research has discovered the continuing power of a personal invitation. Scott McConnell, executive director of Lifeway Research, noted in his book, *Together: The Power of Groups*, that personal invitations play a large part in whether guests will attend a group. "Almost half of churchgoers who participate in a small group or class joined that group because the leader (17%) or member of the group (30%) invited them. This fact alone reinforces the value of relationships in encouraging behavior change. Joining a group is a change in practice. Relationships are the most effective way to get others to join."[7]

Invite People to Take Next Steps

A few decades ago, Bible study groups were the front door to the church. People would attend a small group study before attending a worship service. That process, however, got turned upside down. Today most adults will visit a worship service long before they ever visit a group Bible study. Worship services feel safer to guests—no one asks them to pray out loud, they do not have to interact with people, and they can remain anonymous until they are ready to reveal themselves. They can also experience the "microwave" version of church; they are done in about an hour and can get on with their day.

People need help taking next steps. I recently led a training event for a church in Florida and was fascinated with a question they'd plastered throughout the church building. You could not turn anywhere without seeing a sign, poster, or banner with the words, "What's Your Next Step?" I thought it was a brilliant question because the answer is different for everyone. For people who attend worship only, their next step is to connect with a smaller group of people—a Bible study group. Once a person has connected with the church through worship and Bible study, their next step might be to take a midweek class or more intensive Bible study. For people who have done all these things, their next step would be to serve in a ministry or go on mission. Next steps are different for everyone.

You would assume that people would know the next steps they should take, but they don't. The average person who attends your church's worship service may not know their next step; so tell them! Pastors can help by saying, "I'm glad you are here today. If you have not connected with one of our small group Bible studies yet, let us help you do that today." Communicating the next step is one of the most helpful ways to invite people to connect with your church's Bible study groups.

Fishing in the Bathtub

For now, let's keep our attention focused on people who are only attending your church's worship service. They have taken what I would call "step 1." They are comfortably anonymous. Still, you and I both know the best thing for them and everyone in their family is to connect with age-appropriate Bible study groups.

Let's say the pastor makes an announcement from time to time that encourages guests and members to take "step 2" and connect with a smaller group of people. Call it Sunday school, LIFE groups, small groups, adult Bible fellowship, community groups, or some other term. Regardless of its name, it is a smaller gathering of people. What can you do to help people take that second step? How can you partner with your pastor? The answer is, "Go fishing in the bathtub."

Let me explain. Your church's worship center is the "bathtub." Each week your church most likely has a certain number of guests who attend worship. Because we tend to be creatures of habit, we practically sit in the same place in the worship center each week. I know I do, and I see others do this every Sunday.

Watch for guests who sit within your "zone," the area around where you sit each week in the worship service. That zone may be two or three rows in front or behind you, or it could be the entire section in which you normally sit. If you spot guests in that area, it is *your* responsibility to approach them before or after the worship service, talk with them, and invite them to be your guest in your Bible study group. Do not assume they will automatically know the next step to take; help them take it.

If you lead your group members to fish in the "bathtub" of the worship center, your group could fan out and cover the entire worship center each week. One group I led did this, and we grew over time by inviting people to join us for Bible study. No other group in the church was doing this, so we took ownership of the worship center and connected numerous couples to our Bible study group over time. An invitation is powerful, so go "fishing" in your worship service for new people

> People need to know they are wanted.

who are potential members for your group. People need to know they are wanted.

Invite Absentees to Reconnect

Some numbers are important to know in group life, and the number fifty is one of them. I wrote about this in a previous book, but it is important enough to bring it up again here. There is a rule of thumb about ongoing Bible study groups that says 50 percent of the group's members will be present on any given Sunday (or the day your group meets). If your group's ministry list has thirty people on it, you will have fourteen to sixteen people in Bible study weekly on average.

The fastest way to grow your group is to reach out to the people who are chronically absent and invite them to reconnect with the group. Sometimes people who have not attended in a while feel embarrassed about coming back. They think the entire church may talk about them and the reasons they have been absent. That is normally not true at all, but in the mind of the absentee, it is a reality. Invitations to parties can be natural times to invite absentees to rejoin the group.

Invite People to Connect through Parties

Parties and other fun gatherings are powerful when used as invitations to help people connect with your group. They help group members and guests make connections with one another. As I have observed Bible study groups over the years, the most popular and fastest-growing groups were the ones that had regular parties and social gatherings. Let's face it. People want to have fun! We all look for reasons to connect. Those who lead groups would be wise to consider the benefit of regular fellowships.

1. *Parties allow you to "connect the unconnected."* Bible study groups often forget about using parties as a tool to connect new people to the group. Effective groups invite potential new members to their fun events. It is not unusual for guests to become part of the group before they have an opportunity to connect with the group. People need to connect emotionally and relationally to a Bible study group before they ever attend a single Bible study. Make it a habit to invite potential group members to every party, fellowship, and social gathering. Parties are not just for the group's members; they are for the "not yet members," too. Parties are to groups what on-ramps are to freeways.

2. *Parties allow you to reach out to chronic absentees.* You know that awkward feeling you get when you are about to send an email or call a chronic absentee? You might ask yourself, *Will they respond negatively because I haven't reached out to them sooner? Why didn't I call them when they were absent the first time or two?* It's a lot less awkward to reach out to chronic absentees with an invitation to the group's next fellowship rather than seeking to discover why they've been absent for so long. "Hey, John, I just want you to know we'd love to have you and Jennifer come to our cookout this Saturday afternoon," or "I just want to know if we can save you a spot at our bowling night this Friday night?" Those phrases are much easier to say than, "Hey, we've noticed you've been absent from the group for a month? Is everything okay?" Use a party as a reason to reconnect people to your group.

3. *Parties help your group members connect relationally outside of the group's Bible study.* When your group gets together for a party, you get to know people in ways you cannot in a Bible study setting. People tend to "let their hair down" in a setting not as formal as a Bible study group. The person you had labeled as a stoic might turn out to be the life of the party.

If your group is not in the habit of scheduling regular times for fellowship, there is no time like the present. Schedule some now and ask group members to place them on their calendars. Here are a few ideas to get you started:

- Go bowling.
- Eat lunch together after church once a month.
- Attend a play.
- See a movie together.
- Have a picnic in the park.
- Host a cookout.
- Start a supper club that meets weekly, monthly, or bimonthly.
- Schedule a progressive dinner in homes of group members.
- Take a short road trip or a day trip.
- Visit a museum.
- Go to a ballgame.
- Visit a local festival. (I have taken groups to Moon Pie festivals, banana pudding festivals, and yes, fainting goat festivals.)

The 1:1 Rule

Your group needs one simple tool to be effective in inviting people to connect with your group, and that simple tool is a prospect list. If your church uses software to track attendance, chances are it includes prospects on your group's ministry list. If it does, you are miles ahead!

You can manually keep track of your group's prospective new members by keeping a physical or digital list, whichever you prefer. I typically use a digital list, but you may not. Back in the day, I used a small card file box that held three-by-five or four-by-six index cards to keep information about prospects. I used a physical card file to track prospects when I worked as a clothing salesman years ago. It was not fancy, but it worked.

The 1:1 Rule says that you need one prospect for every group member present. Today the group I am a part of has about twelve people in attendance. According to the 1:1 Rule, we should have a prospect file of at least twelve people.

The prospect file is of no use if a group does not work its file. Every time there is an occasion to get together, whether it is for fun, for Bible study, or for ministry, potential new members should be included. I have seen many groups over the years forget to invite prospects to Christmas fellowships, day trips, and other events to which they would have likely said yes.

Invite New People with the 3X Exercise

Bible study groups may or may not see a steady stream of guests. It varies from church to church. If groups do not see a steady stream of guests, there is a solution to enlarging the pool of potential new members. The 3X exercise says that your group members know, on average, three people who are not connected to a church or to a Bible study group. If groups average ten people, each group knows about thirty people who are potential new group members. Once a year, group members can be asked to write the names of those three people, plus their contact information, on index cards. A church that has fifty adults in groups would discover 150 new people to invite to their Bible study groups. A church that has 150 adults in groups would discover 450 prospects. We should note that this does not include potential new members who are discovered in the church's worship service or through events like fall festivals, Easter services, and others.

As we consider the essential task of inviting people to become disciples, we have asked whether we are praying for lost persons, spending time with them, and inviting them to connect (and reconnect) with the group. All of this is leading up to the last and most important question in this section. We will cover that in the next chapter.

Stop and evaluate your group again. If your scores are not as high as you would like, do not despair. You are identifying places where you can lead your group to do better. This is a guilt-free exercise. There is no condemnation here. When I look at my golf scorecard after a round, it hurts sometimes. I can immediately see where I need to improve. But that is the goal—to get better! Only by being honest about your current state can you discover where you need to shore up your weaknesses. How is your group doing at inviting new persons to connect with the group? Rate your group below.

NEW SCORECARD FOR GROUPS					
		GRADE			
	INVITE PEOPLE TO BECOME DISCIPLES	A	B	C	D
5	Are prayers focused on the lost?				
6	Are group members eating with "sinners and tax collectors"?				
7	Are new persons invited to connect with the group?				
8					

Main Ideas

1. Invitations are powerful. More people will be a guest at your group's Bible study if either the group leader or members of the group are regularly extending invitations for people to come and be a part of the group.

2. There are people in your church's worship services weekly who are potential new members for your Bible study group. Identify them and extend an invitation for them to be a guest at your group's Bible study.

3. Your Bible study's members know people who are not connected to a church or a Bible study group. Together, you can discover many new potential group members by using the 3X exercise.

Questions for Discussion

1. Where could your group find new members? Besides "fishing in the bathtub," where might you discover people who would benefit from being connected to your group?

2. If invited guests showed up, would your group be ready to welcome them by having extra study guides, extra chairs, name tags, and other things to make their experience a good one? What could the group change before the next time it meets so that guests feel welcome?

3. What will you say if the people in your group are not excited about newcomers? How can you lead them to be open, friendly, and welcoming to new people?

To-Do List

1. Order a box of five hundred business card-sized invitation cards (multiple companies online do this inexpensively). Include the name of your church, its address, and the times for worship and Bible study. Include the location of your group as well. On the reverse side, have an area with blank lines for group members to write their names and contact information. Give ten cards to each group member and encourage them to invite people to your group's Bible study.

2. Purchase stick-on "Hello, my name is . . ." name tags, and ask group members to wear them weekly. This will help group members call guests by name when they attend one of the group's Bible studies.

3. Enlist a person or persons to serve as greeters for your group. Their job will be to look for, welcome, and relate to all guests who attend your group's Bible study. Greeters should introduce guests to other people in your group, offer to sit with them in the worship service, and invite them back to the next study.

Chapter 8

Are Group Members Initiating Gospel Conversations?

―――――――――――――――⌄―――――――――――――――

Evangelism and discipleship are two sides of the same coin; both are needed to make disciples. Jesus told the church to "go and make disciples," which involves sharing the gospel, but He also told the church to teach new believers to obey. Some groups do one of those at the expense of the other. The emphasis in some Bible study groups has become a desire to see group members "go deeper." Those groups love digging into the Word of God. They may have an affinity for going through the Bible verse by verse, no matter how long it takes. For these groups, the formula for group life is:

Discipleship = Knowledge

The problem with this is that one day the group looks up and there are no new disciples in it. The group quit being outward facing long ago, and evangelism ceased. Deep Bible study was overemphasized. These groups would do well to come back to the middle and find a balance between evangelism and teaching. Groups that turn inward often overemphasize the discipleship part of group life.

I have had the privilege of leading training events for pastors and group leaders across this country and enjoyed interacting with these "spiritual frontline workers." When I train Bible study leaders, I like to ask, "What is the purpose of a Bible study group?" Though it is a simple question, I always get a wide variety of responses.

The missing element in the answers I receive is the real reason groups exist. *Groups exist to make disciples.* Making disciples starts by praying for people and sharing the gospel with them. It often includes building relationships with these people. Once a person accepts God's offer of forgiveness, we must teach them obedience. Jesus was exceedingly clear about this.

As we continue to create the new scorecard for groups, we must ask, "Are group members initiating gospel conversations?" If the answer is no, don't get discouraged. We simply need to find ways to help groups share the gospel. Sharing the gospel is God's design for reaching the world with the good news. People who are disciples articulate the gospel to people who are not disciples. New disciples are made, and the process repeats.

> Groups exist to make disciples.

If you are a believer, you are the result of this process. Someone shared the gospel with you in a way that resonated with you. God's Holy Spirit convicted you of your need for forgiveness, and you accepted His offer of salvation. Praise the Lord for all the believers who have come before us because they passed the gospel message along to us through many others.

Why Aren't We Sharing the Good News?

If the good news is so good, why don't more people talk about it with friends, family, and acquaintances? After all, we talk about everything else. When it comes to discussing the gospel, however, we are much more hesitant to initiate a conversation. There are a myriad of reasons, but they can be summed up in a few key statements.

1. Lack of practice. Recently, I went to a local golf course to play an eighteen-hole round. I always arrive early and hit a small bucket of practice balls. I practice a few times each week, so I do not feel the need to hit a hundred balls before I tee off. Once I hit twelve to eighteen balls, I am normally ready to go to the first tee box. One particular time when I was on the practice range, another player was hitting balls next to me. I took note because he had purchased a large bucket of balls and was whacking away at them as fast as he could. He had obviously not practiced his golf game in a while, and he was trying desperately to work out some kinks in his swing. He and his group were called to the first tee, which was in view of the practice area, so I turned to see how he hit his tee shot. With a mighty swing of the club, he only caught the top of his ball and it rolled about fifty yards. His body language said it all. He did not walk off the first tee box with any amount of confidence. It was going to be a long day for this poor fellow. The lack of practice in both golf and evangelism will affect a person's confidence. If a person feels awkward and underprepared, he might avoid either activity altogether. Because many Christians do not regularly have gospel conversations, their lack of practice leads to a lack of confidence, which leads to a lack of sharing.

2. Fear. This may be the biggest reason people hesitate to share the good news. Feelings of awkwardness birth feelings of fear, and fear leads to hesitancy. What do people have to fear? They fear not knowing answers to questions the other person may ask. Our minds think up a dozen straw-man questions we may not be able to answer. A Christian might feel hesitant to tell the other person that without Christ he is headed to hell. In today's culture a believer might fear telling another person the gospel is exclusive. Declaring that there is no other way for a person to be saved outside of faith in Christ is not exactly a popular message.

3. No plan. When I have an opportunity to share the gospel, the last thing I want is for the other person to feel like he is on the receiving end of a sales pitch, so I do my best to let the conversation happen organically. Some believers, however, need a presentation framework for sharing the gospel. It might be the Roman Road, One-Verse Evangelism, or some other way to communicate the gospel. If believers knew in advance what they might say to another person about Jesus, they would be much more inclined to speak up.

> Because many Christians do not regularly have gospel conversations, their lack of practice leads to a lack of confidence, which leads to a lack of sharing.

4. Feeling an unreasonable responsibility for the response. Some Christians take on too much responsibility for the other person's response to the gospel. "What if I say something wrong, and they get turned off to the gospel? What if I can't answer their questions, and they reject me and the message?" I remind myself that my responsibility is to speak up and leave the results to God. By sharing the gospel, I am obedient to do what God has asked of all believers.

5. *Friends and family know us too well.* It is one thing to share the gospel with a stranger. It is something quite different to share the gospel with someone who knows us. Perhaps we think the people closest to us will not accept the gospel when they evaluate our life. They have seen us at our best, but they have also seen us at our worst. Satan likes to remind us of our worst moments, so we feel inadequate, and even a little hypocritical, in sharing the gospel.

Three Important Things Every Believer Needs

If the new scorecard for groups asks us to evaluate whether group members are having spiritual conversations with lost persons, we should equip those group members to share the gospel. In my experience, group members know they should share the gospel, but many do not feel ready or able to do so. We can help them by leading them to know three important things.

First, group members need to know how to tell their own stories. In the past I have helped group members write out their testimonies (stories). A person's spiritual story is composed of three things:

- Their life before becoming a disciple
- How and when they accepted Christ as Savior
- What life has been like since becoming a disciple

People start with big bullet points and then fill in more information as they reflect on the events of their lives. When they get their thoughts in order, they write out their story. It does not have to be long, but it should include the three things above. When these come together and the person can articulate the story in a way that makes sense, they have a message that can be shared from memory at any time and any place.

Second, group members need to know the basics of the gospel. There are many ways the gospel can be shared. The ABC method is easy to remember—Accept, Believe, Confess. I like One-Verse Evangelism. With this method, a person memorizes Romans 6:23 and learns to draw a simple diagram. Lifeway's ongoing Bible study curriculum has a gospel presentation on the inside cover of every edition. It is there to remind people of a way to share the basics of the gospel quickly and clearly. If you are a group leader and you want to improve your group's score in the important category of evangelism, teach them simple but effective ways to verbalize the good news.

Third, group members need to hear how fellow group members have shared the gospel. One of the best things to boost the confidence of your group members is to ask one of them to tell what happened the last time they shared the gospel with someone. As group members hear about those encounters, they will live vicariously and put themselves in the presenter's shoes. Over time, group members will be encouraged to step out in faith just like their fellow group members have done. It is one thing to hear the pastor talk about a time he shared a verbal witness with a person; it is something quite different when group member hears the story of a peer who shared the gospel. It helps all group members think, *If God gave me that opportunity, too, I could share the gospel just like so-and-so did.*

Practice, Practice, Practice

Practice makes perfect. You may recall that earlier I said that people often do not share because they have not practiced. One of the best things a group leader can do is to guide his or her people to practice on each other. PGA professionals know they must devote significant time to practicing their craft. *Golf Digest* reported, "In a day, the average tour pro spends about three to four hours concentrating on the full swing and an equal amount of time on the short-game. But tour pros are not just beating balls or blindly rolling putts. They make their practice productive by using props—shafts, yardsticks, and other devices—to check their alignment, their ball position, their swing plane, their putting path. Sometimes it is with their teacher, most often with their caddie, so they have another set of eyes to check them. This is work."[8]

If a golfer never practiced but suddenly found himself with an invitation to play in a tournament, how well do you think that might go? Not well at all.

Suppose a Christian never practiced sharing his spiritual story or the basics of the gospel and suddenly found himself with an opportunity to do both with someone who came across his path. How well might this go for them? Probably not so well, either.

The big difference in the illustration above is that whenever someone shares the gospel, he has a secret ally—the Holy Spirit. He leads and guides people into truth, and He convicts them of sin. The encounter has the possibility of ending with the person accepting Christ as Savior, even though the Christian was not fully prepared to do his best.

The point is that practice matters. Practicing gospel conversations before the opportunity arises makes a dramatic difference in the confidence level of the person doing the sharing when the time comes. Savvy group leaders will always give their group members opportunities to practice on each other from time to time. Think about how this might be done in a group:

- The group leader announces that today, as a
  part of the Bible study time, group members
  are going to share their spiritual stories with
  one another.
- The group leader divides the group into
  two-person, same-gender teams. The two
  people take turns sharing what life was like
  for them before coming to Jesus, the circumstances surrounding their conversion experience, and what life has been like since they
  became disciples.
- After an appropriate amount of time, the
  group leader asks the two-person teams to
  switch roles so that the person who has ini-
  tially listened now shares the gospel with the
  other person.

When this is repeated over time, group members learn
that sharing their story or a gospel presentation is not all
that scary. And when they do this for real, they will have
some "spiritual muscle memory" to fall back on when they
get nervous.

Tyler's Story

On a Tuesday afternoon a few years ago, the phone rang
at the church office where I served. It was someone from
Lifeway Christian Resources calling. The person on the
other end was Wayne Poling, now a dear friend and father
figure to me in ministry.

Wayne was leading a training event in Austin, Texas,
and one of the conference leaders suddenly had to bow out
because he had received a cancer diagnosis and his doctor
wanted him to begin treatment immediately. With only a

little over a week before the event, Wayne called me and invited me to drive down to Austin from the Dallas-Fort Worth area and lead four workshops the following weekend. I accepted.

Before leaving town, I told my wife that I was going to take my golf clubs and play a round of golf somewhere in the Hill Country, the beautiful part of Texas around the Austin area. I went by our bank's ATM on my way out of town and withdrew $100 to cover my round of golf.

When I was about halfway to Austin, which was a three-and-a-half-hour drive, I began to feel sick. My nose started to drip, and my throat became sore. A terrible headache set in, and by the time I got to my hotel, all I could do was stumble into the room and collapse on the bed. Whatever happened, it felt like I had been run over by a train.

The next morning I missed my tee time. I slept right through it. I did not eat a thing all day, and around three in the afternoon I drove to the host church and set up my room along with the rest of the trainers who had flown in from Nashville, Tennessee. I was the only non-Lifeway employee on the training team.

Wayne suggested that the group go out to dinner together, but I declined. I was still feeling run down, and I was going to have a long day on Saturday. After my decline, I drove back toward my hotel. But then it hit me. I had not eaten all day. So I decided to stop and eat something before heading to bed early.

The first restaurant had more than an hour wait. It made sense. It was after five on a Friday night in Austin, Texas, after all. I was determined to eat something, so I stopped at a second restaurant and discovered they had an even longer wait. After my second attempt to find a meal, I decided to give up and go back to the hotel where I thought that I could, at least, buy some cheese crackers out of the vending machine and make that my dinner.

As I pulled into the hotel parking lot, I realized it shared a parking lot with a Bennigan's restaurant. Giving it the old college try, I walked over to the restaurant to see if I could get in. Same story. All full. And that is when the miracles started.

As I turned to leave the restaurant and go back to the hotel, the hostess caught me by the sleeve and said, "Look, you are a party of one, and normally we'd seat you in the bar, but I have a four-top that just opened up, and I'm going to put you there" (a four-top is a table with room for four people). They should not have sat me there by myself. I should not have jumped past all the people waiting in the lobby. But God had plans for me and my waiter.

My server, Tyler, a young twenty-something student at the University of Texas, walked over to my table to take my drink order. "How are you, sir?" he asked. I replied that I was okay, and I asked him the same question. His response was intriguing. "I'm not so great." When I asked why he was not doing well, he explained that a large party of ten had just left the restaurant (he had been their waiter) and $100 was missing. He was not sure, but he thought it fell out of the leather holder that all restaurants bring you when you get the bill. His manager explained in a no-nonsense way that Tyler would be responsible for making up the $100 that was missing. Tyler said it would take him the rest of the evening plus all day Saturday to make that up, and he could not afford it because he was moving out of his apartment on Sunday for a less expensive place to stay. Even though I thought it was bad luck, I went ahead and ordered my food.

Then I had this random thought. *I wonder if I was being scammed?* Was this kid giving me a sob story just to get me to tip bigger? Had he really lost that much money? I was skeptical, so I began to listen to him as he spoke to other guests at the tables around me. Not one time did he repeat his story of the lost money. *Hmmm,* I thought.

As I sat there eating my meal, I heard a still small voice speak to me. Not in an audible voice, but it was His voice for sure. The Holy Spirit reminded me, "You know that $100 you brought to play golf? Give it to Tyler." I got goose bumps because I felt the strong presence of the Spirit. I pondered what had just run through my mind and thought, *No way.* After all, I could play golf on the way home or even play at a course back home that was nicer than I might normally play. I deserved to be rewarded for helping Lifeway, I reasoned. So I just kept eating.

Don't judge.

Tyler kept circling back as good waiters do, and I decided to ask him a question. "Tyler, did you ever find the missing money? Did anyone turn it in?" His answer was no. Again, I felt the nudge from the Spirit: "Give your money to Tyler."

Tyler brought me my bill, and I paid by credit card. He brought the leather holder back to the table, thanked me for dining there, and went about waiting on his other tables. I signed the receipt, then turned it over, and I wrote Tyler a long note. I shared the gospel with him in that note. I left him my name and phone number. And I put the $100 in the leather holder. On my way out, I ran into Tyler (on purpose). I asked, "Did that $100 ever show up?" He said it had not. And then I said, "It just did." I placed the leather holder in his hand and walked out of the restaurant and headed to my hotel.

Hang with me because this gets even better.

Halfway across the parking lot on my walk back to the hotel, I heard footsteps running up behind me. I turned around to see Tyler standing there. He had the most shocked look on his face I had ever seen. He held up the leather credit card holder and asked, "What is this?" I told him if he had read my note (which he had) he already knew the answer. I told him that I believed with all my heart that God told me to give him the $100 I had in my wallet because he needed it. He cried. I cried. And then he ran back to the restaurant because he had left his tables unattended. I went on to my hotel room and thought that was the end of the story.

Then another miracle happened.

I completed my workshops on Saturday and felt exhausted but good. The attendees had been engaging, and I had finally begun to feel better physically. I had a good meal the night before and a good night's sleep. I had left Tyler with $100, and it was almost time to drive home.

A lady from Lifeway, one of the assistants on this training trip, came by my classroom as I was leaving. She handed me an envelope and said thank you to me for filling in on such short notice. I asked her what was in the envelope, and she said it contained a check. "A check for what?" I asked. She went on to explain that Lifeway did not expect me to spend a weekend training people and not get paid. There was a check for $400 in the envelope—$100 for each of the four workshops I taught. *No one told me I was getting paid to do this!* I thought I was helping Lifeway and that I would benefit by getting some conference experience. You just can't make this stuff up. I cried the whole way to the car. I had given Tyler my $100, and God turned around and replaced it with $400. Amazing.

And the story gets better. . . .

The next week I was back in my office at the church and my cell phone rang. It turned out to be Tyler. Tyler said that he got my name and number off the back of the receipt from Friday night. He told me how grateful he was for the help, but he got me all choked up when he explained what God had truly done that Friday night.

Tyler said that for years he had been angry at God and had walked away from Christianity, the church, and Christians. His mother and father had some difficult days in their marriage, and a pastor (according to Tyler) encouraged one of them to leave the other. Tyler blamed the pastor, the church, and God for the demise of his family when he was a teenager. He had been bitter toward God for years.

But Tyler said that the simple act of kindness, that $100 gift, was the way God broke through to him and spoke to his heart. He said he realized now that not all pastors were like the one he blamed for ruining his parent's marriage. It was probably a good thing I signed the receipt, "Pastor Ken."

But wait. The story gets even better.

Fast-forward about eight weeks after my encounter with Tyler. It was spring break in my kids' school district, and our family traveled in a caravan with four other families from our church. We were on our way to go skiing in New Mexico. It was a Sunday morning, and we were somewhere in the Texas panhandle. The phone rang. It was my pastor back in Grapevine, Texas. Because it was about 10:30 a.m. on a Sunday morning, and because my pastor's name was on the caller ID, I thought, *Oh no, I must have forgotten to do something.*

"Hey, Pastor Gregg," I said. "Is everything okay?" Gregg assured me that all was well. He said, "There's someone here who wants to talk to you."

"Hey Pastor Ken!" he said. "This is Tyler from Austin." He went on to say, "I'm here with my *entire* family. We all drove up yesterday so we could be here today to surprise you and worship with you at your church. Ken, we are all back in church and back to the Lord now. We wanted to celebrate that with you. It all started with that $100 gift." I about wrecked the van I was driving because I could hardly see the road through my tears.

There are people just like Tyler all around you, me, and our group members. We encounter them at school, at work, on trips to the grocery store, or even places like Bennigan's. They are everywhere, and they are far from God for whatever reason. Many people have not had a great experience with churches, with Christians, and may have given up on God. Maybe they are angry about how life has turned out or because of the untimely loss of a loved one. Who knows why people shake their fists at God?

Bible study groups exist for people like Tyler. Members of our Bible study groups can learn how to speak up when God opens doors. They can share their spiritual story, the gospel, or a hundred bucks. Those of us who lead groups can help our group members articulate the gospel as they share their spiritual journey with others. We will leave the results up to God.

So, what is our role in all of this? Speak up! Once we do, God says, "I'll take it from here."

As the new scorecard grows and expands, the second section looks like the one below. These are the new ways we must think about how our groups are really doing. Bible study is more than just teaching. It is more than what happens on a Sunday. I trust that you are beginning to sense that a teaching ministry is based on more than just how many people attended the group.

Are the members of your Bible study group inviting others to become disciples? Are they initiating gospel conversations? You will know if they are because they should be telling the group about them. If things are quiet, chances are they are not articulating the gospel like they could. They need your help—a little nudge—to begin taking advantage of the opportunities God gives them daily to share the gospel. Rate your group on the next page on line 8. How are they doing? How would you rate them?

NEW SCORECARD FOR GROUPS				
	GRADE			
INVITE PEOPLE TO BECOME DISCIPLES	A	B	C	D
5	Are prayers focused on the lost?				
6	Are group members eating with "sinners and tax collectors"?				
7	Are new persons invited to connect with the group?				
8	**Are group members initiating gospel conversations?**				

Main Ideas

1. The gospel is advanced when Christians share the gospel in their day-to-day relationships. It is vital that believers know how to share their faith.

2. The reasons Christians do not share the gospel regularly include fear, not being able to articulate their testimony, and not having a simple plan for sharing the basics of the gospel.

3. People all around us, like Tyler, are in desperate need of the gospel. God is at work, placing people like Tyler in your path each day.

Questions for Discussion

1. How might group members realize the importance of sharing their spiritual stories with others?

2. What is your go-to gospel presentation? Why do you prefer that one?

3. Have you had a "Tyler" moment in your life? What happened? How did God use that gospel-sharing encounter to change you or the other person?

To-Do List

1. Lead your Bible study group members to write their stories (testimonies) and practice telling them to each other in groups of two or three people.

2. Identify a gospel presentation that is brief and effective. Teach it to the members of your Bible study group. Occasionally give them opportunities to practice presenting the gospel to one another in groups of two or three people so they feel prepared and ready for an encounter with an unbeliever.

3. Watch out for the Tylers in your life with whom you can share the gospel. As you discover these individuals, add them to your prayer list.

Measurement 3

Form Deeper Relationships

Chapter 9

Are Groups Organized to Care for People?

The first-century church had a problem.

The church was growing rapidly, and it was reaching different people groups. This was not the problem. As these groups became one in Christ, however, a problem arose that threatened to destroy the unity that was enjoyed up to that point. Even though the church distributed food to widows, some of the women were being overlooked. Feelings were hurt. Anger may have set in. Complaints arose. Here is what Luke records in Acts 6:

> In those days, as the disciples were increasing in number, there arose a complaint by the Hellenistic Jews against the Hebraic Jews that their widows were being overlooked in the daily distribution. The Twelve summoned the whole company of the disciples and said, "It would not be right for us to give up preaching the word of God to wait on tables. Brothers and sisters, select from among you seven men of good reputation,

full of the Spirit and wisdom, whom we
can appoint to this duty. But we will devote
ourselves to prayer and to the ministry of
the word." This proposal pleased the whole
company. So they chose Stephen, a man
full of faith and the Holy Spirit, and Philip,
Prochorus, Nicanor, Timon, Parmenas, and
Nicolaus, a convert from Antioch. (vv. 1–5)

The group of believers had grown exponentially, and
the church struggled to keep up with the needs of the
members. Thankfully, the leaders decided to involve others
in caring for people. When a proposal was made to recruit
a group of men to oversee the daily distribution of food, it
pleased everyone. More leaders meant that more care could
take place. Needs would be met, and people would not be
overlooked.

At some point the needs of people outgrow the ability of
a single leader to meet them. More people had to be recruited
to help care for others. Some scholars believe this Acts 6
passage shows us the genesis of the role of the deacon. One
thing is for sure in this biblical account. When more people
got involved and lent a hand, the quality of care went up
significantly.

Today many Bible study groups are led by a single leader.
This person tends to be one of the busiest people in the
church. In a previous book, David Francis and I wrote about
the three roles every group leader has: teacher, shepherd, and
leader.[9] We said in that book that it is rare to find a person
who excels in all three roles. Leading and teaching a group
by yourself is an exhausting challenge.

When it comes to caring for people in Bible study groups,
teachers need help. Unless the group is a microgroup, the
span of care becomes so large that one person cannot do it

alone. That person needs others in the group to help care for the other members. This is where care groups come into play.

What Are Care Groups?

Care groups are groups within a group. They are a place for group members to be subdivided and cared for by a fellow member of the group—a care group leader. This subgroup has a unique function within the larger group. "A care group is simply a grouping of people for the expressed purpose of making regular contacts for prayer, communication, and the discovery and meeting of needs."[10]

Care groups care. It is as simple as that. Care groups are a way some Bible study groups have chosen to make certain that every person (not just regular attenders) is always cared for. A care group leader encourages his or her small group to pray for one another and to meet one another's needs in practical ways. A care group leader would ideally contact the six to eight persons in the group weekly. As needs are discovered, the care group leader would then mobilize the rest of the group to meet those needs. It might be the meeting of a physical need or a spiritual one.

How Many People Should Be in a Care Group?

The right size for a care group is six to eight people. In some groups that would mean each group has three or four couples, or a mixture of couples and singles, depending on the makeup of the group. There are advantages to making care groups gender-specific, placing men in groups and women in groups. You reduce the possibility of an infatuation between two people of the opposite sex. The conversations can also be more honest and open in single-gender groups. Care groups work because care groups are small. When you see care groups approaching the size of eight to ten members and beyond, you should start thinking about creating another group and redistributing the people.

When Do Care Groups Meet?

Some Bible study groups allow time in each Bible study session for care groups to gather and pray, talk, and plan for ministry. Sometimes a care group will plan a monthly or quarterly fellowship for themselves. Care groups also plan a time when they serve together in the community, normally on a Saturday. Each care group is autonomous and meets when it is best for its group members.

Who Can Be a Care Group Leader?

Anyone with a shepherd's heart and a desire to see people cared for is a good fit for this role. Having organizational skills is a plus. A person who takes commitment seriously is also a good candidate for this role. It also helps if a care group leader regularly attends. It is hard to care for people if you are not there to meet with them (or at least see them) weekly. Ideally, a care group leader connects with group members each week. That can be done in person, on the phone, by text, or some other form of digital communication. Whatever the method, consistency is important.

How Are People Divided into Care Groups?

The group leader along with the care group leaders should sit down and make a "draft." The group's ministry list should be viewed, along with each person's attendance record. Each care group should have a combination of regular attenders (70 to 100% attendance), people that attend occasionally (30 to 70% attendance), and some people who are infrequent or chronically absent (0 to 30% attendance). Each group needs balance so that no one group has all the regular attenders, while other groups have all the absentees.

Essential Tasks of Care Group Leaders

Care group leaders have essential tasks they should accomplish as part of their ongoing ministry. These tasks help ensure that people's needs are met, which gives the group's teacher a chance to focus on creating engaging Bible studies. The group leader's time can be spent in study and prayer, much like the apostles did in Acts 6. The basic job description of a care group leader is as follows.

1. Contact every person, every week. This is the heart of the work of a care group leader. Every person in a care group should receive a phone call, an email, a text, or some combination of these. Do this for group members who were a part of the larger Bible study group meeting, and do this for those who are absent.

2. Discover needs, meet needs. This is also crucial in the life of a care group. As needs are discovered, members of the group should be mobilized to meet those needs. You may be surprised how excited and eager people will be to help their fellow care group members. If a need is too large for one care group to meet, the care group leader should ask for help from other care groups.

3. Recognize special days and events. Care croup leaders should remember their members' special days—birthdays, anniversaries, and even difficult days such as the day a group member's child or parent died. Care group leaders can also encourage the celebration of special occasions, such as a job promotion or a recognition received in their workplace.

Five Kinds of People Who Need Care

There are different kinds of adults who participate in groups, adults with specific and unique needs that deserve attention. The new scorecard for groups asks the question, "Are groups organized to care for people?" Caring includes meeting the needs of five kinds of people.

1. Absentees. Every group has a certain percentage of people who are absent whenever the group gathers for Bible study. It is not uncommon for up to 50 percent of group members to be absent each time the group meets for Bible study. An effective care group leader will not only rejoice over those who attend regularly, but he or she will reach out to those who don't. A quick phone call, an email, or a visit to the person's home can help reconnect an absentee to the group.

2. Prospects. Unless the Bible study group is closed to new members, every group should have a prospect list. I recommend that a group have one prospect for each active member. It is wise to include potential new group members (with their permission) in care groups even before they officially join the church or the group. This becomes another important step in the process of assimilation. Potential members should always be invited to fun social activities and community service project days sponsored by the group.

3. People in crisis. It is a given that if you have a group of people coming together to study the Bible, things are going to get messy at some point. People will experience the ups and downs of life, and you may find yourself in the role of a "first responder." A job loss, the sudden death of a loved one, or a crisis with a child may bring a group member to a moment of crisis. Groups never intentionally ignore people in need, but sometimes a person in a crisis is accidentally overlooked (that is why it is vitally important that every person be included in a care group). How many people have left a church because they perceived that nobody cared about them?

4. *Associate group members.* Associate group members are people who leave groups to serve others by serving somewhere in the church. Perhaps they felt called to teach a group of pre-schoolers, kids, or teens. The best thing you can do is make sure they are not forgotten! Pray for them often. Invite them to every fellowship your group sponsors. Send them information about the group's studies and activities. And by all means, keep them in a care group! Associate members need to know they have not been forgotten. They also need affirmation for using their spiritual gifts elsewhere in the church.

5. *Regular attenders.* It is easy to forget about these people, but do not! Although the guest, the person in crisis, the associate member, and the absentee all need time and attention, so do loyal group members. It is easy to let these good group members go unnoticed, but these people need an encouraging word from time to time, too. Thank them for their regular attendance and for being a stabilizing force in your group.

Resist the Temptation to "86" People

One time when I was in the process of ordering a hamburger, I asked the waitress if she could "86" the onions. She looked at me like I was from another planet. "I don't know what that means," she said. I explained that the term is slang for "leave it off" or "remove it." Evidently it came in vogue in the 1920s and '30s, but the exact origin of the phrase is in dispute. Still, I have always liked the way it sounds.

While serving full-time as a groups pastor on a church's staff, one of my Bible study groups got really organized. The group's record-keeping assistant called the church office one Monday morning to ask me to "86" several couples from the group's ministry list. "We have never seen these people," she said. "They are messing up our percentage of attendance! If they were not on our list, we could have almost 100 percent attendance every week." I sighed. I told her that we only remove people from a group's list of members for one of three reasons:

- The person died.
- The person told us to remove them.
- The person joined another church.

The lady could not honestly say this was the case, so I explained why the people she asked about would continue to be left on the group's ministry list. I encouraged her to reach out to these couples and see why they had been missing from the group for so long. She was not very happy with me but said she would call them. And to her credit, she did. The responses were mind-blowing. It changed her perspective about dropping people versus caring for them.

The following Sunday, two of the couples came to the group's Bible study! During the group's prayer time, one of the two wives admitted that she and her husband had been away too long and felt awkward about showing up, but the phone call from the group's administrative assistant encouraged them to start attending again. She went on to describe some of the struggles they had been having, and I later heard that people in the group felt guilt for leaving them abandoned for so long. Everyone learned the importance of caring for people that day. The group members continued to reach out to other absentees, and they embraced the couples who returned. The group reorganized itself into care groups and became one of the best groups I have ever seen.

The new scorecard for groups asks us to consider whether people in groups are forming deeper relationships. A step in the right direction is to make sure groups are organized to care for people. How would you say the groups in your church are doing? How about your group? Do you resemble the first-century church leaders who were overwhelmed with caring for people in need? Do you need to reorganize your group to be more effective at meeting people's needs? We can all do better in this area. Caring for people starts with being organized and intentional.

Rate your group below. What score would you give them? Is the group organized into microgroups we call care groups? If yes, are those groups truly caring for people? If you cannot give your group an A or B rating, that is okay. You have identified an area in which the group needs to improve. No group is perfect, and every group has room for improvement!

NEW SCORECARD FOR GROUPS					
		GRADE			
	FORM DEEPER RELATIONSHIPS	A	B	C	D
9	Are groups organized to care for people?				
10					
11					
12					

Main Ideas

1. Sharing the load of leadership is good for everyone. Leaders receive the help they need, and group members use their gifts to serve others.

2. Groups that are organized to care for members experience a sense of community and connection. Fewer people "fall through the cracks" when a group is organized to care for its members.

3. Groups must care for a variety of people. Only organized groups will do this successfully.

Questions for Discussion

1. What would it feel like if you or a family member had a crisis or a need that went unmet by your Bible study group?

2. When was the last time a group of believers met a need in your life and made a difference for which you were grateful? Describe what happened.

3. In what ways would organizing your Bible study group into smaller care groups positively affect the members?

To-Do List

1. Request a copy of the membership role of your group. Divide the group into smaller care groups based on how often the people attend (to make sure that every care group has a balance of regular attenders, semi-regular attenders, and nonattenders). Place six to eight members in each group.

2. Pray about which group members could serve as care group leaders. Look for the ones with the spiritual gift of shepherding, those who are regular in attendance, and those who want people to experience ministry, connection, and a sense of being valued by the group.

3. Host a fellowship at your home to introduce the concept of care groups to your potential care group leaders. Explain the content from this chapter. Invite them to become care group leaders, pray, and set a day and time to get their responses.

Chapter 10

How Balanced Are Connection and Content?

Retired NBA star Charles Barkley is an avid golfer. For years he has been ridiculed by friends, fans, and foes for his unconventional and out-of-balance golf swing. Some have labeled his swing as "choppy." One commentator even joked that Barkley appeared to be having a medical emergency. People have laughed and made jokes at the NBA superstar's expense.

A golfer with a balanced swing creates something visually appealing to behold. The swing is powerful, graceful, and effortless. I watch a lot of golf on television, and my wife wonders how I can sit there for hours. Truth be told, I am observing every aspect of each golfer's swing—the address, the takeaway, the backswing, the downswing, and the follow-through. For me, a golf tournament on television is a learning experience, not just something to watch. I enjoy seeing well-balanced swings of the club.

Over the years, I have worked hard to create a balanced golf swing. In the past I frustrated myself when I hit too far behind the golf ball. I thought it was my clubs, so I bought new ones. Even with a new set of clubs, I was losing a lot of swing speed when I hit behind the ball, which resulted in lost distance. My shots were not crisp, and I could not figure out what I was doing wrong. I watched the pros hit shots that seemed so easy, so natural. I wanted that, too! After I invested in a series of lessons with a PGA teacher, I finally figured out the culprit—a loss of balance. Being out of balance created all kinds of issues for me. When I discovered how to swing my clubs in balance, playing golf became thrilling.

Effective group leaders understand that connection and content must find balance. By connection, I mean the relationships people form in Bible study groups. Some groups are out of balance today. A group can have the best content from the most well-prepared teacher, but if people are only gathering to share an hour of Bible study today only to go back to their separate lives, then something crucial is lacking. Content is important in Bible study groups, but so is connection.

When a group leader knows his group members, content and connection become more balanced. As a group leader prepares his Bible study for the group, his connection to each member helps him frame up the content he wants them to discover. By knowing his group members outside of the Bible study, he discovers ways to connect the content to their life situations.

Is Content Truly King?

Trustworthy biblical content is vital to people and groups. Throughout the New Testament there are admonitions to guard doctrine closely and to beware of false teachers. The content of Bible studies matters deeply.

Still, connection and community are important as well. They are two sides of the same coin. Hear the words of a church leader about the need for content and connection in groups.

> The mood around content is shifting. . . . Yes, content matters because sharing the Word of God matters . . . immensely. However, many Christians now realize they can watch or listen to their favorite preachers, content creators and voices in the world today any time for free. So they do. One approach is to try to equal or match the exceptionally gifted and skilled communicators out there. But for most leaders, that is not a winning strategy. You will not be able to compete. Growing churches (and yes, that includes small and mid-sized churches too) will realize that connection and community will win out over content in the end, and they will focus their resources there. Nobody should be able to out-local or out-community the local the church . . . make the goal connecting with people. When you provide connection (getting to know people, moving them into community, caring for them), it will provide a loyalty and sense of tribe that people can't get elsewhere.[11]

The Side Effects of Imbalance

If content and connection are not balanced, there will be consequences. There have already been consequences in groups that did not maintain this balance. Groups should strive to provide strong, biblically accurate content while simultaneously providing connection for group members.

One side effect of imbalance is sporadic attendance of group members. When content is king and connections between group members are not made, the group Bible study is simply an academic experience. If group members are not able to make friends and establish more enduring, deeper connections with others, frustration sets in. People stop attending. People were made for relationships, and while excellent content is needed, the focus on content should not destroy connection!

Groups should strive to provide strong, biblically accurate content while simultaneously providing connection for group members.

In my early days of ministry, I assumed Bible studies were mostly about the content. I looked for and recruited the best teachers I could find. You know the ones—teachers who could exegete passages and amaze their group members with their biblical knowledge. But even with these tremendous teachers, I began to observe a puzzling trend among my church's Bible study groups. The groups with the most academic and best-prepared teachers were not the ones that always grew. Instead, I watched less gifted group leaders double their groups. What was their secret?

Then I learned a hard truth: *content is not always king.* The groups that grew the fastest and replicated themselves by starting new ones were the groups that played together, prayed together, served together, and did life together. These groups had shepherd-teachers who were perhaps "B+" teachers, but they loved their sheep, and the sheep knew it. That connection made all the difference. Because I have the spiritual gifts of teaching and knowledge, I love good content and teaching it in an engaging way. I hate to say it, but it took me a long time to admit that the relationship side of group life was just as important to group health as was the content side. Groups that find this balance thrive. Groups that are focused almost exclusively on content sometimes struggle to attract new members because relationships are not valued as much as the content being studied. When this happens, there is little follow-up with absentees, and fellowship times are undervalued, as well.

A second side effect is that "2:00 a.m. friends" are not made when content is more valued than connection. We all need a few more of those kinds of people in our lives—the ones you can call any time of the day or night. Think about some of the good friends you have made along the way as you connected with Bible study groups over the years. Chances are you are remembering their names and seeing their faces right now. You probably still know them and interact with them in person. Maybe you keep up with them on social media because there is a great physical distance between you now. Those friendships are often birthed in a group setting.

A third side effect is that people come to believe that group life is about the one hour of study. When content is king, group leaders focus on the time when the Bible is taught. I once inherited a group leader when I transitioned to the second church I served. He was an excellent teacher who was knowledgeable about the Bible. People wanted to be in his group. There was just one problem. This teacher did not allow people to speak! He had so much content to deliver each week that he didn't want group members slowing him down. Members of the group could not ask questions, nor could they add their comments or connect the content to their lives. Because content was king, the group leader dominated the group's Bible study time. People learned things, lots of Bible factoids, but the group ultimately disintegrated when he left town for a new job opportunity. There just was not enough "relational glue" to hold the group together. Maybe content isn't as kingly as some groups think it is.

Creating Connection

If connection is needed in groups (and it is), the question becomes, How do we create opportunities for people to know one another and build relationships? The people who attend Bible study groups can find some of the best Bible teachers online. Local group leaders will not compete with those giants of the Christian faith in knowledge, presentation, and communication abilities, so they must compete on a level where they have a chance of winning. For local leaders that level is the connection level. Great online Bible teaching is a stroke, swipe, or click away. When it comes to connecting people, however, the local church has the upper hand. Groups and group leaders can win every time.

"I can walk with God without other believers"

From online survey for SWBTS Center for Revitalization of 2,500 churchgoers Jan. 2019

Strongly Agree	Somewhat Agree	Neither Agree Nor Disagree	Somewhat Disagree	Strongly Disagree
36%	29%	15%	11%	9%

But connecting people is not without its challenges.

According to Lifeway Research, Christians do not necessarily drift toward connection. Scott McConnell, executive director of Lifeway Research, stated, "We must raise the priority of investing in relationships with each other. We must do a better job of explaining why. Today, two-thirds of churchgoers believe they can walk with God without other believers. They are missing the fact that we know God better together."[12]

Connect people during the Bible study time. If group leaders allow people to tell their stories from everyday life, group members will make connections with one another. Asking open-ended discussion questions that are crafted to draw out personal stories and experiences helps people connect relationally. I have seen friendships form when one person shares something that has taken place in their life, and another person in the group responds with "I went through something similar!" The two group members start talking after the Bible study ends, and soon a beautiful friendship has formed.

Connect people in smaller microgroups. Small, same-gender groups that intentionally form within a Bible study group are terrific for connecting group members. People will be much more inclined to move into a three- or four-person group when they are familiar with the other people. Forming these smaller groups within a group is a clever way to help people move into even smaller and tighter relational spaces. Microgroups (which I'll touch on later) deepen relationships, inspire spiritual growth, and provide a place of higher accountability to help Christians walk with Christ daily.

Connect people through parties. I have already touched on this in a previous chapter, so I will not belabor the point again. Just remember that everyone likes a fun gathering. Absentees are more likely to reconnect with the group at one of them, and as people have fun, visit with one another, and connect outside of the group's Bible study, deeper relationships will form.

Connect people through ministry projects. Have you ever been on a weeklong mission trip? My family and I participated in several annual mission trips to Juarez, Mexico, with a busload of people from one of our former churches. By the end of the week, we had grown close to our fellow missionaries, many of whom we did not know prior to the mission trip. Once we returned home, people continued building relationships that started on the trip to Mexico. All that to say, the same thing happens when groups decide to minister regularly in the community. Those shared ministry days—Saturday at the local clothes closet or crisis pregnancy center—help people connect in ways they would not by just sitting in a Bible study group.

Connect people through prayer. As groups pray, smart group leaders place people into smaller triads or quads and invite them to pray for one another. If a Bible study group is arranged into care groups, those groups can pray together before, during, or after the Bible study time is completed. Sharing prayer time is another way for people to deepen relationships and learn what is taking place in the lives of others.

Movement Precedes Balance

Connection and content must be balanced in the church's Bible study groups. But before there can be a balance, groups must have people to balance. Your church's worship service may be described as a "step 1" event. It is where most people's journey into a church begins. A "step 2" ministry is your church's Bible study groups. If someone takes step 1 and attends worship, you would hope they take one more step and attend a Bible study group (that's the movement). Remember this: *programs do not connect people; people connect people.* Moving people out of the worship service and into a small group is essential for connection to take place. This is the kind of movement churches need to foster.

My wife and I are avid moviegoers. We have a pass that allows us to see up to three movies a week. When we go to our local theater, we associate with the other people who are there to see the same movie we are viewing. Associating with people is different from participating with people.

Think about how we associate with our fellow moviegoers. We buy the same kinds of snacks, we watch the same five or six previews before the actual movie begins, and we laugh and cry at the same parts of the movie. But when it's all over, hundreds of us disburse and go our own ways without any participation. There's no real connection, only association.

> Programs do not connect people; people connect people.

In a similar way, worshippers experience this. Worshippers sing the same songs, they listen to the same message from the pastor, and they hear the same announcements. This creates an event in which people associate with one another, just like at the movie theater, but people do not *connect* with one another. Connection requires something more than just sitting and listening. For me to connect with others, I need a time and a place where I can engage with people in a smaller group. We must talk. We need opportunities to share what we're thinking. What people really need is to move beyond association and into a time of participation.

Before connection can happen between people in a group, people must move into a group. In my experience, there are strategic ways a church can create movement from the worship service to groups. These things take place in the church's weekly worship service and nudge people into a smaller environment where they can participate with others. Some churches have discovered success by doing any of the following things during the worship service:

1. Pray for a different group and its leader weekly. Remind the congregation and guests of any online group options your church provides.

2. Interview an individual or a family about the things they enjoy about their Bible study group.

3. Schedule a commissioning service where you pray for all the teachers at the start of a new Sunday school year (usually in August).

4. Preach a sermon series on the importance of groups, Bible study, and connecting with others.

5. Use the worship bulletin to feature a group and its teacher each week. Be sure to provide a short bio on the group leader, where the class meets, the Bible study curriculum used by the group, etc.

6. Create a special registration card in which people can specifically request to be con- nected to a Bible study group.

7. Preview an upcoming session's study theme to create interest (e.g., "Next week our groups are studying X," or "We're about to start a six-week study on Y, and it's a good time to be out guest in one of our Bible study groups").

8. Preach a sermon series that aligns with the Bible study series used by your adult groups

and encourage guests and unconnected members to participate in a group.

9. Encourage guests to stay and connect with a Bible study group while they are on campus.

10. Encourage worshippers who are online to take next steps and connect with an adult group.

11. Encourage time-compressed people to attend a Bible study group instead of the worship service. I have served with several pastors who have encouraged people to get involved in a smaller group if they only have one hour to give on Sunday mornings. Pastors understand that people are more likely to be around for the long haul if they are in a group.

12. If you are the pastor, share a personal testimony of what you are learning in your Bible study group. You can set a great example for others to follow by being in a small group, too.

I mentioned Charles Barkley's horrific, out-of-balance golf swing earlier. You can search the Internet and see examples of his swing, or rather, his former swing. You see, Mr. Barkley decided to do something about it in recent years. The swing he has today is much more fluid and balanced than ever before. *Golf Monthly's* online magazine reported, "Once unable to produce a flowing swing, Charles Barkley revealed his drastically improved action at Alabama's Greystone Golf & Country Club during the Regions Tradition Pro-Am on Wednesday. . . . 'I told you,' Barkley claimed to Bo Jackson, seen in the video hugging Charles seemingly in disbelief. 'I'm going to play great all day, Stan Utley got me fixed.' Barkley hired professional trainer Stan Utley to improve his handicap, which is reportedly now down to single digits. Renowned for his less-than-textbook technique and signature hitch in the downswing, the NBA Hall of Famer managed to smoothly strike through the ball, pleasantly surprising everyone watching."[13] Barkley found new balance, and it changed his golf game. With a little effort, Bible study groups can find new balance between content and connection.

We are well on our way to creating a new scorecard for groups. When people visit Bible study groups, they expect trustworthy content. They also expect excellence in the way it is communicated to the group. *The unspoken hope is that in addition to great content, they will also experience great connection with others.* People want and need friends. Are your church's groups delivering on that? How about your group? How would you rate it on the scorecard below? When new people visit your group, would they say that content and connection are balanced?

NEW SCORECARD FOR GROUPS				
		GRADE		
FORM DEEPER RELATIONSHIPS	A	B	C	D
9	Are groups organized to care for people?				
10	How balanced are connection and content?				
11					
12					

Main Ideas

1. The content of the Bible study must be balanced with the community aspect of the group. Great content is essential, but so is great community. People need both.

2. Groups need regular fellowship opportunities. Relationships act like glue that will bind people's hearts to one another.

3. When content and connection are out of balance, it will have adverse effects on the group. If people don't feel connected and fully assimilated into the group, attendance will be sporadic, deep friendships will not be formed, and group members will come to believe that the emphasis is on the one hour of Bible study time.

Questions for Discussion

1. How balanced are content and connection in your Bible study group? What evidence is there to support that assessment?

2. Looking back at the ideas for increasing connection in Bible study groups, which ideas are the "lowest hanging fruit" that could be implemented in your group?

3. If the pendulum has swung the other direction and connection has overtaken content, how can a Bible study group move back to the middle and do a better job studying God's Word together?

To-Do List

1. Enlist a person or persons to create and schedule the fellowship events sponsored by your group. Ask them to make sure the group gets together once a month (this is preferable) or at least once a quarter.

2. Schedule a "Tables of 8" event to help group members get to know one another more deeply. To do this, ask any couple or persons interested in participating to give you their name and contact information. Randomly place them in groups of 8. Instruct groups of 8 to meet once a month for four months. In the first month, one of the couples (or two singles) act as host for a dinner gathering. This can be at a restaurant or at their home. The two people sponsoring the fellowship event can add games or icebreaker activities. Before the night is over, another two people volunteer to sponsor the same event next month but at a different home or restaurant. Do this for four months.

3. Use teaching options like buzz groups and triads or quads (three- and four-person groups) to boost connection and discussion (rather than asking the entire group to respond to a question, the group leader divides the group into smaller ones and then asks these smaller groups to respond). This is good for learning, but it also fosters and strengthens connection among the people. Many people are hesitant to speak up in a larger group, but those fears diminish when there are only three or four people in their discussion group.

Chapter 11

Do Newcomers Experience Biblical Hospitality?

The year 2010 was painful for the Braddy household. During the middle of the Great Recession, I left a church staff in Texas to move to Nashville. Lifeway offered me a position from which I could influence the Bible study materials of millions of people weekly. I felt God's call and could see His hand in the process, so we left a church family we loved dearly. We also left our families and moved eleven hours away. I did not think it would take us the better part of our first year in Nashville to find a new church home. But it did. That was the worst part.

For almost twenty years, I served on two church staffs in Texas. As we moved to Nashville, we were excited to attend and belong to any kind of SBC church we wanted. Would we join a megachurch or a small church? Would the church have Sunday school or home groups? Would the congregation sing hymns, choruses, or both? Would the church's members dress casually, or would they dress up? The sky was the limit. Sundays were filled with anticipation, hope, and excitement. We looked forward to seeing where God would lead us.

And then the excitement wore off. Sundays became painful.

My wife and I committed to worship with a congregation each week. We also committed to go to whatever Bible study group was offered for our age and demographic. I know that most people visit a church's worship service for a long time before they connect with a group, but we wanted to make new friends, so we did it the old-fashioned way: we visited Bible study groups weekly.

I wish I could tell you that our experiences in groups were awesome that year. They were not. We sat in groups on many Sundays, and no one spoke to us. *And I mean no one.* The people carried on conversations with one another as they moved around the room with coffee in hand. I am sure people recognized us as guests, but they did not approach us before or after class. This might sound like I am making it up, but I'm not.

We visited a group at a megachurch for multiple Sundays leading up to Christmas that year. That was about six months into our search for a new church home. We attended the potential new members' class and heard all about the church's history, ministries, and plans for the future. The only thing that remained was for us to connect with a group of adults. We felt like we were making progress, having visited one group for multiple Sundays. And then it happened—the slow-motion train wreck you cannot stop watching.

On a Sunday morning in mid-December, Tammy and I sat in a circle with that Bible study group—the one we had visited multiple times. We had not made any deep connections yet, but the people seemed friendly, and we thought we could make new friends in time. The teacher taught the Bible study that morning, and afterwards the group finalized plans for its annual Christmas party and ornament exchange. *Now you're talking!* I thought. Tammy and I loved those kinds of parties. We attended every one of them at our previous churches. *This is it,* I thought. The moment we really connect with this group. It will be like the Bible study groups back home that held these same kinds of Christmas parties!

The group leader and his wife (we were sitting right next to them in the circle that morning) reminded the group at whose home they would meet, but they didn't invite us. We had tried so hard to connect with these people. I thought we were on the verge of finding a new church home, but I realized we would have to start all over. Visitors were not included. This party was for "the group," and we clearly were not part of the group. It was the last day we visited that church.

I will come back and finish this story a bit later in the chapter. Thankfully, there is a happy ending, but it did not happen at this church. I have told this story in conference and training settings, and I almost always have several people who come up to me at the break and say, "I had the same experience trying to connect to churches where I live." That makes me sad. People should not have to work so hard to connect with Bible study groups. Groups should realize the importance of showing biblical hospitality to strangers.

> Groups should realize the importance of showing biblical hospitality to strangers.

All Groups Turn Inward

Groups turn inward over time, which makes showing biblical hospitality to guests more difficult. I have experienced this in groups I've led and some I've attended. As a group leader, I've worked hard to keep the group's focus on reaching new people and welcoming guests. Maybe you have had a similar experience, too? Why do groups do this? Why do they turn inward? Why don't they remain ready to connect people to the group? Why is biblical hospitality so lacking? I believe I have finally figured out why this happens.

Time is not your friend if you are in an open group. By definition, a group is an open group if it anticipates that guests might be present any time the group meets. After a group has been together about eighteen months, it typically begins to turn inward. The inward turn happens because the group members have cared for one another, prayed for one another, served with one another, and partied with one another. They have done just what the church asked them to do. The by-product of group life is a slow but gradual inward turning. The group members almost never notice it, but guests do. Can you imagine the inward turn that groups take when they have been together for five to ten years? It becomes difficult to assimilate new people into those groups. This is why churches must start new groups!

Unless a group's focus is on reaching and welcoming new people, the group will miss opportunities to practice biblical hospitality that leads to the assimilation of strangers. The main hope for combatting the inward turning is a group leader who understands the true mission of the group. *The mission is to reach people and make disciples.* A part of that mission happens during the group's Bible study time. A group leader who reminds his or her people to be warm and welcoming to outsiders is posturing the group to assimilate new people. If you have not been a guest in a group lately, you have probably forgotten how awkward it is to be a guest. Biblical hospitality goes a long way in breaking the ice. Sadly, most groups could do a lot better in this area.

When a group turns inward, it must work hard to correct it. Groups can do several things to communicate that they want and need newcomers. First, they wear name tags. My friend David Francis wrote about wearing name tags in every one of his books about Sunday school. I suppose I am picking up that mantle. I have asked the groups I've led to wear name tags. One group member groused, "Why do we have to keep wearing these stick-on name tags each week? We know who we are." I reminded him that guests do not know that. I asked my people to wear name tags as a visible sign that we are outwardly focused and expect new people to show up weekly. Second, a group should have extra chairs so that guests have plenty of places to choose from. There is nothing like being a guest and having to sit on the front row of a group. Trust me, I know. Tammy and I visited several groups in our yearlong quest for a church home, and they only had enough chairs for the group members. I can recall one time when a group member had to run down the hallway and borrow two chairs from another group just so we would have a place to sit. A friend of mine recently told me that he'd visited a Bible study group but was told he could not sit in the seat he had chosen because it was "being held" for a group member who had not arrived yet.

Finally, groups that are postured to connect people always have extra personal study guides. Tammy and I visited a church in northern Mississippi one Sunday, and the teacher taught a Bible study series that my teams produce at Lifeway. I saw extra study guides on a table behind him, but we were never offered one (even though everyone in the group had a

> The mission is to reach people and make disciples.

copy). We followed along in our Bibles, but it was awkward when he referred to something in the study guide and we had no way to participate. It is the little things that say, "We want you here," and "We want you to connect with us."

Showing Biblical Hospitality

I once spoke to a group of church leaders at a training event in Pensacola, Florida. A topic that I was asked to address was that of biblical hospitality as seen and experienced in the church but especially in Bible study groups. I defined biblical hospitality in three ways. Think of these as the three legs of a stool. All are important. Take one away and the stool will not stand.

> If we are going to practice biblical hospitality, we must treat strangers and friends in the same way.

1. Biblical hospitality means we value people as unique creations of God. If we are going to be hospitable to strangers, we must remind ourselves that individuals who visit our groups are one-of-a-kind creations. Those persons were created by God, and there is no one else like them on the planet. When you have that mindset, it is easier to treat them as honored guests. Even if they do not look or dress like members of the group or speak well or have the biblical knowledge the rest of the group members have, that does not diminish the fact that they are fearfully and wonderfully made.

2. Biblical hospitality means we treat strangers and friends in the same way. If a friend of mine showed up in a Bible study group I lead, what would I do? That's easy! I would smile, shake his hand, find him a seat, give him a study guide, introduce him to people already in the room, and introduce him to the entire group as we began our Bible study time. I am confident that does not happen when guests are among us. If we are going to practice biblical hospitality, we must treat strangers and friends in the same way.

3. *Biblical hospitality means we welcome new people into our homes, our churches, our groups, and our lives.* It should come as no surprise that a Bible study group gets no extra points for being friendly to a guest, right? Newcomers expect friendliness to be a hallmark of churches and groups. What guests hope and long for are ways to connect relationally with others. Group members accelerate that process when they invite the stranger to have lunch with them after church. Everyone eats Sunday lunch! Biblical hospitality is shown when the newcomer is invited into a group member's home, and biblical hospitality takes place when we invite the person into our lives.

The new scorecard for groups reminds us that practicing biblical hospitality is something that helps people form deeper relationships with believers. How would you rate your group? Do newcomers feel like they are old friends with people in your group? Do guests return and ultimately join your group, or do you see a steady stream of newcomers who do not end up connecting with the people? Using the new scorecard on the next page as you have in previous chapters, rate your group. Once you do that, respond to the questions below to help you process what you have read.

NEW SCORECARD FOR GROUPS				
		GRADE		
FORM DEEPER RELATIONSHIPS	**A**	**B**	**C**	**D**
9	Are groups organized to care for people?				
10	How balanced are connection and content?				
11	**Do newcomers experience biblical hospitality?**				
12					

Main Ideas

1. Biblical hospitality must be a hallmark of Bible study groups. Unfortunately, not all groups act in a welcoming way toward newcomers.

2. All groups will turn inward in time. It takes strong, vibrant leadership to keep a group's attention focused on reaching people who are not a part of the group.

3. Biblical hospitality is evidenced by the way we invite strangers into our groups, our churches, and our lives.

Questions for Discussion

1. How friendly is your Bible study group? Now ask that question again from the vantage point of a stranger who has recently visited it. Would that person say the people are friendly, or would they say the people are friendly toward one another?

2. How might groups raise the "friendly quotient" and help strangers feel more like family? What can your group do

immediately to help create a more biblical environment that is kind toward outsiders?

3. Does someone in your group have the spiritual gift of hospitality? Who is that person, and why do you believe that gift is present in them?

To-Do List

1. Ask your group members to wear stick-on name tags weekly.

2. Invite every guest and potential new group member to any fun fellowship event your group schedules.

3. Enlist a person with the spiritual gift of hospitality to be your group's greeter. Their role will be to pay special attention to any guest who attends your group's Bible study.

Chapter 12

Are Microgroups Strengthening Relationships?

Jesus had a microgroup. We may think we stumbled into something brand-new when we talk about helping people gather into smaller groups, but the truth is, Jesus did this in the first century. It worked out well.

Jesus spent most of His days living life with His twelve disciples. Occasionally, He spoke to the masses, like He did during the Sermon on the Mount. But that was the exception and not the norm. His typical day started with Him retreating to quiet, lonely places to commune with His heavenly Father. Then, as the day progressed, He and His disciples traveled the Judean countryside. Sometimes He stopped the group when a teachable moment presented itself, like when He overheard His men arguing about who was going to be the greatest in His kingdom (Luke 22:24–30). On other occasions He taught in synagogues, or He responded to a person's need for healing. All the while, His disciples were there observing Him, listening to Him, and being prepared for ministry when He was gone.

And then there was His microgroup: Peter, James, and John. These men were a smaller subset of His group of twelve disciples, a group within a group. He decided to invest additional time into these three men. They heard teachings and saw things the other disciples did not. It was a special group that had special times with the Savior. Jesus could have kept all the disciples together without meeting with this microgroup, but He chose this strategy to develop Peter, James, and John.

A Rose by Any Other Name

This may be the first time you have heard the term *microgroup*. It is exactly what it sounds like: a smaller group. You may be more familiar with the term *D groups* (short for "discipleship groups"), or the term *pods*, depending on where you are in the country. I doubt there will ever be "one term to rule them all," but the purpose of these groups is similar. People who participate in these microgroups are at a place in their growth as disciples where they highly value a deeper walk with Christ. That growth is fueled by a deeper walk with fellow believers. When I use the term *microgroup*, I'm referring to a small three- to four-person group that meets together for an agreed-upon time. After that time ends, the members of these microgroups often replicate the process when each member invites others into the same kind of relationship for a year or so.

What Goes Around Comes Around

Today, church leaders are rediscovering the benefits of microgroups in strengthening relationships and deepening discipleship. The idea and practice of microgroups is ancient, but the benefits are as relevant today as they were in the first century. These groups don't replace the need for a believer to be in a larger group of Christians for Bible study, but they do provide a place where growth and relationships are accelerated.

In a recent online panel discussion with Lifeway's small group champion, Chris Surratt, church leaders from the western part of the United States told stories about the way they use microgroups to connect people. These church leaders wanted to see people join groups, but they related the difficulties they experienced in getting people to commit to attend a group where the people are strangers to them. People who are not accustomed to taking part in a Bible study group can be hesitant about meeting with people they do not know well, and these church leaders explained how they experienced success in gathering people into groups of three or four people who already have relationships with one another. They found that people were willing to be connected to a microgroup if they knew one or more of the people in it. The deeper level of discussion, the intentional relationships, and a higher level of accountability not possible in larger groups were all part of what made this attractive to them.

Friends or Friendliness?

When people attend a Bible study group, they expect it to be friendly. When a group does not deliver a warm and inviting experience for its guests, it disappoints potential group members. People expect churchgoers to be friendly; we don't get any extra points for showing biblical hospitality. But at the same time, people are not just looking for friendly groups; they are searching for friends.

But don't take my word for it.

Do an online search for the California Mermaid Convention. You will find people looking for groups with whom they can share experiences related to things they mutually value. Swimming around a hotel pool with a mermaid (or merman) fin around my legs does not sound appealing, but it is to the hundreds of people who show up for that annual convention. Search online again using the term "BronyCon." You will discover an annual convention of grown men and women who are fans of My Little Pony. Search again for a Star Trek convention, and you'll find thousands of people coming together to meet the stars of the show, dressing up in

> People are not just looking for friendly groups; they are searching for friends.

costumes, and talking with one another about their love for the crew of the *U.S.S. Enterprise. People want to connect.* They want to share life. For believers, microgroups are the perfect place for deeper connection as they simultaneously deepen their discipleship experience and growth in Christ.

It is one thing for a person to be a member of a Bible study group. It's quite another for them to find that deeper level of friendship. In countless Bible study groups, people may be members, but they are not truly connected to others at a deeper level. Assimilation is missing whenever someone does not have that 2:00 a.m. friend they need.

Microgroups are another way churches can help people become fully assimilated. Keep in mind that "assimilation is more than just becoming a member of a group. In fact, a person may be a member but never be assimilated into the body. The goal is to help people feel they are wanted, that they belong, and that they are needed."[14] If you were to survey people in your church, you'd find that some would admit to being lonely in their groups. Even though they are surrounded by people, they have yet to discover the sweet spot of group life, the microgroup.

Attitude of those not in groups toward attending a small class or group through their church in the future

26%	68%	6%
Unlikely to consider regularly attending	Open to the idea of attending	Actively looking for a small class or group to attend

A recent Lifeway Research survey discovered that 68 percent of the people who are in churches are open to attending Bible study. Another 6 percent are actively seeking to connect with a Bible study group.[15] When combined, that means 75 percent of the people in our churches are open to connecting to a Bible study group. Once we help them find an appropriate group, their next step is being nudged toward giving their time to be a part of a microgroup. That is where groups, and our churches, get very "sticky."

A Group within a Group

While church leaders can encourage members and guests to join microgroups, a more practical way to go about this is to use the church's existing Bible study organization to champion the formation of microgroups. Group leaders can encourage the formation of microgroups within the groups they lead. People already know one another, and these small pods will often form organically as friends link up for a slightly deeper and different experience than they get in the larger class or small-group experience.

Microgroups 101

A microgroup has a few important characteristics that differentiate it from the larger Bible study group it is a part of. The goal is similar in both groups—to make disciples and provide a place for deeper relationships. Microgroups help people experience spiritual transformation and growth over time, with replication of the experience being a primary reason for the group to exist.

Microgroups are less formal and less didactic than an ongoing Bible study group. The microgroup is a highly relational group, a healing place, and a source of encouragement.

> People should feel the freedom to bare their souls to their brothers and sisters in microgroups.

It is a place to find strength and to remain faithful to Jesus as one of His disciples. It is also a place where honesty and vulnerability are necessary. People should feel the freedom to bare their souls to their brothers and sisters in microgroups. In this place Christians can confess their sins to one another. Each microgroup is unique, of course, but generally they have these characteristics:

- *People are invited into the group.* In an ongoing Bible study group, anyone is welcome to attend at any time. It is different in a microgroup. The person who initiates the group invites a few same-sex individuals to meet and grow together. Therefore, a microgroup is a closed group that does not anticipate new people being added once the group begins.

- *There is no set time limit for weekly microgroup meetings.* Groups self-determine how long their microgroup meets each time the group gathers. It depends on the desire and the schedules of the group members. Some will meet on a lunch hour, while others will meet early for breakfast or coffee. Some might meet on a weeknight after work. But unlike on-campus groups, there is no time constraint other than what the members impose on themselves.

- *Microgroups determine how frequently they meet.* Some groups meet every week, while others choose to meet biweekly or once a month.

- *Many microgroups commit to meet for one year.* Meeting for one year provides enough time for relationships to deepen while allowing enough time for group members to learn how to lead a microgroup of their own. While some group members will want to continue meeting, it is preferable for group members to know on the front end that the group is not ongoing. These groups are meant to "make disciples who make disciples." At some point the microgroup ends, the group members disband, and each person recruits new people to a microgroup of their own.

- *The ultimately goal is to start new microgroups.* In 2 Timothy 2:1–2, you can see four generations of disciples. Paul was a disciple first,

Timothy received the gospel from Paul, Timothy entrusted the gospel message to faithful leaders, and those leaders passed the gospel along to a new generation of disciples. Microgroups can follow this biblical pattern by stating at the outset that in one year the group is expected to disband so that each person can start up another microgroup with new people.

- *A higher level of commitment is expected.* Group members are expected to attend the group's meetings, to be honest and open about their struggles, and to be willing to be held accountable to walk with Christ daily.
- *Microgroup leaders focus on fruit, not facts.* In a Bible study group, "getting through the lesson" tends to be important. Teachers have a lot of information to convey, and they want group members to experience and know the things God is teaching them as they prepare. In a microgroup, the focus is on how God is using the group, the group members' personal study times, and their devotional lives to grow and transform them into more fully devoted followers of Christ. The maturation of the believer, especially as seen in the fruit of the Spirit, is imperative.
- *Each member of the group can and should lead over time.* Although there is a leader, shared leadership is highly valued so that apprenticeship takes place and group members gain experience and confidence to lead a microgroup of their own one day. Multiplication is assumed and desired.

- *There is as little hierarchy as possible.* Microgroups keep the "organization" flat. People are equals; the group leader might be thought of as "the first among equals," but group members need to see themselves as leaders in training, not dependent on a "teacher" or a "leader" to do the work for them.
- *People should accept the organic nature of microgroups.* You have no way to force anyone into a microgroup. Stress the importance of those groups, describe what takes place, and talk about the benefits. Realize that the formation of microgroups within your larger Bible study group may take time, and that's okay.

Resourcing Microgroups

Lifeway has created a significant discipleship tool called the DDG (Daily Discipleship Guide). It is a study guide for members of adult and student Bible study groups and is designed to help people in Bible study groups establish themselves into microgroups. If your group prefers a book-by-book study, there is Explore the Bible. Some groups may prefer a more topical approach to studying the Bible. And for those, Lifeway offers Bible Studies for Life. And finally, The Gospel Project provides a third approach to navigating the Scriptures chronologically. Each of these popular series has a Daily Discipleship Guide that contains three important features:

1. The group Bible study (thirteen in all).
2. Five daily studies that group members complete throughout the week following each group Bible study.

3. A microgroup feature that helps facilitate discussion among two to four same-sex people.

If a church decides to provide each adult group member with a Daily Discipleship Guide, each group member is positioned to have everything they need for a successful microgroup. They would experience the group Bible study. They would have their own "God and me time" each day as they discovered different aspects of the Bible passage studied by their group. And finally, the microgroup feature would give them discussion questions built on their week of learning and discovery. The DDG aligns the group's study with the individual's daily time in the Word.

Starting Microgroups

Paul and Timothy could be considered a microgroup of two; Priscilla, Aquilla, and Paul were a microgroup of three. They had to start somewhere, and so do the microgroups your group might foster today. If your group does not have these smaller gatherings of group members yet, you can follow these steps to get them started.

First, if you are a Bible study leader, form a microgroup of your own. Invite two or three others to begin a discipleship relationship and close the group when you have three others who commit to be a part of your new microgroup. Let them know that the purpose of this group is not to be together forever but for the group members to deepen their relationships with one another while also deepening their walk with God. A good microgroup leader will express his or her desire for the participants to start microgroups of their own in the future.

Second, if you are a group leader, talk openly with your entire Bible study group about the benefits of committing to be in a microgroup. Let them know you have previously started a microgroup and enlist a member or members of that group to speak on behalf of the benefits they are receiving by being in the microgroup.

Third, announce that you and your microgroup members are starting new groups and that everyone in the group will be invited to take part in one. Be sure there are microgroups for men and for women. As new people join the larger Bible study group, inform them of the existence of microgroups, and get them thinking earlier rather than later about creating margin in their schedules to be part of a microgroup.

Microgroups are an effective way for people to deepen relationships, challenge one another, and provide a high accountability setting for people who want to go deeper in their walk with Christ. Is your group using microgroups to help people strengthen relationships and make disciples? What grade would you give your group today?

NEW SCORECARD FOR GROUPS					
			GRADE		
	FORM DEEPER RELATIONSHIPS	A	B	C	D
9	Are groups organized to care for people?				
10	How balanced are connection and content?				
11	Do newcomers experience biblical hospitality?				
12	**Are microgroups strengthening relationships?**				

Main Ideas

1. Jesus had a group of twelve disciples, but He also had a smaller group of three into which He poured His time and energy. Today we are rediscovering the power of a microgroup for strengthening relationships and accelerating growth as disciples.

2. People are searching for friends. They associate with groups of people who have similar interests, lifestyles, careers, and more. People want and need connection.

3. Microgroups help people build deeper relationships, provide a higher level of accountability, and prepare members of those small groups to launch microgroups of their own.

Questions for Discussion

1. In what ways do you see people forming groups that are focused on interests of the group members? What does this say about our need to be with others who like and value the things we do?

2. Look back at the Microgroups 101 section from the chapter. What are some of the main advantages you see in forming microgroups within your Bible study group?

3. How has you experience in a microgroup been helpful to you in your growth as a disciple?

To-Do List

1. Continue learning about microgroups by doing some research for yourself. See what else you would add to the

description and benefits of using microgroups within your Bible study group.

2. Identify two people from your Bible study group (same gender) and invite them to begin a one-year journey in a microgroup with you. Make sure they know the goal is not to stay together forever but to launch and lead a microgroup of their own when the yearlong time commitment has ended.

3. Talk to your Bible study group about the benefits of microgroups. Answer their questions, overcome objections, and start a few groups.

Engage in Acts of Service

Chapter 13

Are Groups Making a Difference in the Community?

A cts is an exciting book of the Bible. Throughout it, you will find the church fighting for its life, and its people, at times, narrowly escaping death and persecution, and at other times, not. You will see the kingdom of God advance, and you will see the gospel move out from Jerusalem to Judea to the uttermost parts of the world just as Jesus promised it would. Before much of that happened, there was Acts 2. This chapter chronicled a special part of the story of the Jerusalem church.

> Everyone was filled with awe, and many wonders and signs were being performed through the apostles. Now all the believers were together and held all things in common. They sold their possessions and property and distributed the proceeds to all, as any had need. Every day they devoted themselves to meeting together in the temple, and broke bread from house to house. They ate their food with joyful and sincere hearts, praising

God and enjoying the favor of all the people.
Every day the Lord added to their number
those who were being saved. (Acts 2:43–47)

You have read these verses before, I am sure. But did
you notice what happened because of their newfound faith?
These first-century Christians became overly generous, selling property so that others could benefit and have their needs
met. They ate and prayed together and were unashamed of
their faith in Christ. Their faith compelled them to meet
publicly in plain sight. The community in which they lived
took notice. These Christians were strange people indeed!

Notice how the community responded to the way the
first-century Christians lived out their faith in Christ. The
Word says that believers went about "enjoying the favor of all
the people." Believers made a difference. Their reputation for
love and good deeds became well known. These first-century
Christians were no stumbling block to the gospel. In fact,
their good works drew attention to Christ and showed the
community how different life could be with Jesus as Savior.
Being a Christian was not limited to a particular time of the
week in those days. Christianity made a difference *every* day
in how people lived.

"You Don't See the Job"

"Bible study isn't about what happens from 9:00 a.m. to
noon on Sunday," said a friend of mine. He went on to say,
"If you think Bible study is about Sunday morning, then you
don't see the job." Those words were spoken a long time ago,
but I can still hear them like they were said yesterday. Those
words have guided my philosophy on what a teaching ministry should be.

Over the years I have told group leaders that the real work of leading a group begins when church dismisses on Sunday and continues until bedtime the following Saturday. A teaching ministry must not be confined to a Sunday morning experience. This means that the work of Bible study groups is constant. We must stop seeing a teaching ministry as just a Sunday morning event. It is much more than that.

In a survey by Lifeway Research, executive director Scott McConnell and his team discovered that one reason people join Bible study groups is to help others. "It is possible that our communication about groups spends too much time telling people to just do it or join because of what you will get. Joining a group needs to equally be about what you can give to others."[16] Is your group making a difference in the community? Are you acting like the early church in Acts 2? I hope so. But if not, don't worry. There's always room for improvement in any group. That is why we are creating a new scorecard for groups. As in golf, you must first identify the parts of your game that are weaker than others and spend focused time improving them.

You Are Now Entering the Mission Field

Have you seen those signs at the exit driveway of churches that contain the words, "You are now entering the mission field"? These signs are there to remind churchgoers that a lost and dying community is all around them. It is a good message that conveys the reality that church members do not have to cross oceans to be missionaries. The community in which your church is planted is waiting to see if you are serious about your faith. Our actions often speak louder than our words.

However well intentioned the people were who placed those mission field signs at the church exit, I often wonder if those signs are making any difference in how churchgoers interact with people in the community. Do people really see their local community as the mission field? Those signs are the last thing people see as they leave the church, right before their attention turns to "Hey, what do you want for lunch?" How often do we just go about our busy lives without doing anything to serve the mission field in our backyards?

Groups Are Making a Difference

The good news is that some groups do treat their community as a mission field. They regularly serve people who live in the community. In most churches those groups are the minority. Just think what could happen if every group in every church took advantage of the opportunities all around them to represent Christ, serve others in His name, and know the joy of dying to self.

One such group I have known for a long time did just that when they decided to adopt the local women's shelter in Grapevine, Texas. The group adopted one woman at a time. These women were often on the run from an abusive spouse or boyfriend and had children with them. This Bible study group outfitted each woman's apartment while she went through the shelter's job placement program. When the program ended and she graduated, this wonderful Bible study group celebrated with her by presenting her with a car! Not a new one, mind you, but a great used car they had purchased and fixed up. The men did the work they could and let mechanics do the rest. It gave each woman a reliable form of transportation. This group did the same thing for multiple women over the years. It was their way of serving beyond the church campus and ministering to people in the community. They made a difference and had a great time doing it. It deepened the relationships between group members as they served.

I have seen other groups adopt schools. They help teachers pack up their rooms at the end of the school year, mentor children, read books to them, or eat lunch with them at an elementary school. Other groups coordinate their efforts with the school's administrators and painted playgrounds, trimmed bushes, and did other physical labor to benefit teachers, kids, and leaders at the school. Still other groups organized backpack and school supply drives annually. They knew how to live out Acts 2.

Thirty Ways Bible Study Groups Can Make a Difference

I recommend that Bible study groups commit to at least one community service day each quarter. This is not a big task, and it gives a nice rhythm of ministry. It also gives groups the opportunity to involve their entire families—kids and teenagers—so they grow up serving others. It is best if these service days are planned well in advance so that people can place them on their calendars. Last-minute project opportunities do pop up from time to time, and a group can get behind them and make them happen at the last minute, but I have found that planning them ahead of time allows for greater participation.

Throughout the course of the year, groups with a quarterly plan for serving people in the community will only need to schedule four events. Here are some of the ways groups can make a difference in the lives of people in their communities:

1. Paint a school playground.
2. Serve at a food pantry by organizing and/or distributing food.

3. Prepare meals at a homeless shelter.
4. Deliver meals to homebound adults.
5. Visit a nursing home and talk with residents.
6. Answer phones at a crisis pregnancy center.
7. Provide in-person counseling at a crisis pregnancy center.
8. Wrap packages for free at retail stores during the Christmas holiday season.
9. Bake goodies and deliver them to first responders.
10. Assemble and take care packages to homebound adults.
11. Mow a yard for an elderly person.
12. Do household maintenance and general handyman work for senior adults.
13. Change the oil and fluids in cars belonging to single moms.
14. Clean up a school's property.
15. Serve lunch to a school's faculty.
16. Assemble personal care packages with toiletry items for a homeless shelter.
17. Schedule a backpack drive.
18. Collect items to fill backpacks.
19. Conduct a diaper drive for a local crisis pregnancy center.
20. Serve as volunteers for the day at your local hospital.
21. Sort clothing at a clothes closet ministry.
22. Collect winter coats for a local ministry to distribute during winter months.
23. Pass out cold bottles of water to random people at a playground or ball field.
24. Work a shift at your local soup kitchen or homeless shelter.

25. Adopt a highway and pick up trash.
26. Sing Christmas carols at a nursing home.
27. Organize an afternoon of board games at a nursing home and spend time with the residents.
28. Beautify or add some landscaping to a school.
29. Buy some coloring books and crayons for kids and leave them in hospital waiting rooms.
30. Sponsor a family in your community and provide Christmas presents and a Christmas meal.

These are just a few ways groups can make a difference in the lives of people in their communities. Groups serve in the name of Jesus, not to call attention to themselves or their churches. Groups regularly serve others because God first served all of us, demonstrating what it means to take the initiative when people have needs they cannot meet on their own.

> Groups regularly serve others because God first served all of us, demonstrating what it means to take the initiative when people have needs they cannot meet on their own.

Every Group Needs One of These

Whether your group is a normative size, like ten to twelve people, or a larger group with many more members, one key leadership position is needed if you want to make a difference in your community. I will say more about this later, but for now, just know that every group needs someone who will take ownership for community ministry.

In a normative-sized group, that person may be the group leader. But in slightly larger groups, someone besides the group leader should step up to serve, involving the whole group in regular ministry to people in the community. A person who has the spiritual gifts of administration and/or helps is ideal for this role. They should have a strong desire to meet the needs of others and to see members of their group use their time and talents to do ministry in Jesus's name. With a little forethought, a community service leader could easily calendar four events per year. Because the year breaks down into four quarters, this makes it even easier to select projects that make sense with the changing seasons.

A Final Thought

We are not the first ones to wrestle with the idea of group members serving beyond the church's address. David Francis wrote about Lifeway's former VP, Dr. Ed Stetzer, in one of his books. Stetzer believes it is important for believers to move out of pews and into circles and then move outward into the community to serve others.

> If Christians are going to effectively engage the world around them, they are more likely to do it with a class or group as the base of operations than with a pew. . . . A Sunday School class is a perfect operating base for fulfilling the Great Commandment and the Great Commission. Most appeals to ministry and missions are either too individualistic or too global. Between "You personally give and go" and "Everybody everywhere

cooperate to support this huge effort" is a sweet spot where a single class or small group, working together, can act "glocally" to accomplish a mission. I believe, along with Ed Stetzer, that this may be a pivotal time for the Sunday School movement. Will it turn inward, as so many movements do? Or will it—through the actions of thousands of individual classes—turn outward to do the things God cares about most, the things Jesus modeled when He walked on the earth, the things the Holy Spirit most enjoys empowering believers to do: seeking, serving, and saving the lost?[17]

I hope and pray that groups will embrace the challenge, responsibility, and joy of serving others in the days ahead. As we create a new scorecard for groups, this is a much-needed addition to group life. Think what might happen if groups everywhere decided to move outward from the church's address and mix and mingle with people from the community. I believe the name of Christ will be lifted, and we will see men, women, boys, and girls come to know Him as Savior and Lord.

How's your Bible study group doing? Do you see evidence that members are making a difference in the community? At present, how would you rate your group's effectiveness in this important task?

NEW SCORECARD FOR GROUPS					
			GRADE		
	ENGAGE IN ACTS OF SERVICE	**A**	**B**	**C**	**D**
13	**Are groups making a difference in the community?**				
14					
15					
16					

Main Ideas

1. Faith in Christ should lead believers to make a difference in people's lives, especially in the lives of people who live in their community.

2. There is a mission field surrounding your church. You can be a missionary to the culture as you and your Bible study group find ways to meet people's needs in your community.

3. Serving the community is made easier if your Bible study group has a person who accepts responsibility to strategize and schedule four service project days per year.

Questions for Discussion

1. What opportunities to meet people's needs do you see in your community?

2. Who in your group would be great at organizing the people to serve others throughout the year?

3. Looking at the section titled *30 Ways Bible Study Groups Can Make a Difference*, which five suggestions are most feasible for your context?

To-Do List

1. Work with your group members to determine a force-ranked list of opportunities for your Bible study group to serve others in your community.

2. Check with your pastor or staff leader to determine if your group has access to any funds designated for ministry to people in the community.

3. Make a list of ways your group members would benefit by having regular opportunities to serve people in the community. How might this also benefit the church?

Chapter 14

Are Group Members Encouraged to Serve in the Church?

As I said at the beginning of this book, engaging in acts of service to others is one of the four measurements on the new scorecard. In the last chapter we observed how groups can serve people in our communities. Now we turn our attention to another aspect of serving: meeting people's needs inside the church.

The key to serving through groups is balance. We want to serve people in our communities, but we also want to serve our brothers and sisters in Christ. If we stress the importance of serving in the community to the detriment of serving others in the church, we will end up with imbalanced group practices.

Catch and Release

I will admit that I am not much of a fisherman. I enjoy eating fish but not catching them. My dad enjoyed getting out on the lake in his boat, and I can remember times when he would bring back fifteen to twenty catfish on stringers. I remember because I got to "help" him clean the fish! If my dad caught a fish, he planned to eat it. For him there was no such thing as catch and release; it was always "catch and keep."

When it comes to Bible study groups, I am a big fan of having a catch and release philosophy in regards to the people in the group. If we are not careful, those of us who lead a Bible study group could develop the same philosophy my dad had: hold onto the ones we catch and do not release any.

One of the greatest signs of group health is when a Bible study group regularly releases people to serve in the church. These groups willingly and happily release adults they have worked hard to "catch." The measure of a great Bible study group is not how large it grows but how many people it releases to strengthen the church's other ministries. Sometimes group leaders want to maintain the size of their groups as if it is some kind of a badge of honor. I have had teachers look me in the eye and say, "Don't come in here and split up my group!" Other group leaders have said to me, "Don't take so-and-so out of my group; I need him here!" It has happened at least once or twice in every church I have served.

> One of the greatest signs of group health is when a Bible study group regularly releases people to serve in the church

This is an area in which we need some new scorecard correction! We should celebrate when people leave our groups to serve. We must realize that the biggest group does not win. I would prefer to have groups on the smaller side but releasing people to serve rather than larger groups where no one leaves.

Adult group leaders are crucial in the process of staffing the various ministries of the church. They play a vital role in keeping opportunities for service in front of their group members. My wife Tammy and I started a new adult group a few years ago, and on day one—launch Sunday—I told the handful of people who came together to start the new group that I expected some of them to step out of our group after a year and go serve in the kids or student ministries. I explained that we are not to "sit and soak." I wanted our group to be the kind of group that was known for "sending and serving." Guess what? One of those founding couples did just that; Mike and Ashley left our group and became "missionaries to kids" by teaching a class of preschoolers. We made sure we stayed connected to them as a group by inviting them to our class fellowships and community service days; we also prayed for them and asked God to bless their teaching ministry.

> The measure of a great Bible study group is not how large it grows but how many people it releases to strengthen the church's other ministries.

Storehouse or Clearinghouse?

During my seminary days, I had a mentor and friend, Dr. Daryl Eldridge. He was my church's minister of education before serving as dean of the School of Religious Education at Southwestern Seminary in Fort Worth, Texas. I invited him to come to a church I served during my early days of ministry and lead a teacher training event one weekend.

He told a group of Sunday school teachers that "Sunday school is not a storehouse; it is a clearinghouse." Those words have stayed with me over the years. I cannot tell you how many times I have repeated them when I have led workshops. My encouragement to teachers has always been to hold onto the people in their groups with a loose grip. Catch and release is the way to go!

Acts 13:1–3 contains some wonderful truths for those adult teachers who struggle to let go of their people. The Bible says, "In the church that was at Antioch there were prophets and teachers: Barnabas, Simeon who was called Niger, Lucius the Cyrenian, Manaen, a close friend of Herod the tetrarch, and Saul. As they were ministering to the Lord and fasting, the Holy Spirit said, 'Set apart for Me Barnabas and Saul for the work I have called them to.' Then after they had fasted, prayed, and laid hands on them, they sent them off" (HCSB).

There are some good reminders about the blessings of "catch and release" from this text. Some of these were pointed out by Dr. Jeff Iorg, the president of Gateway Seminary, in his book *The Case for Antioch*:[18]

1. *The church had many prominent teachers/leaders.* God was specific in calling out Barnabas and Saul to be released to serve elsewhere.

2. *The Holy Spirit told other leaders to set apart Barnabas and Saul.* He did not tell Barnabas and Saul directly. The calling to release the men to serve elsewhere came from other leaders in the church. Sometimes you and I may receive a similar word from the Lord as we observe people in our groups, people God is calling to use their leadership gifts in another place.

3. *Barnabas and Saul chose to be obedient to the Spirit's leading.* These two men chose to leave the Antioch church to serve in new ways. Their obedience and release from the group led to the establishment of new churches on their missionary journeys. The people reached by those new churches would in turn reach more people for the Lord.

4. *Even when the church released two of its best leaders, others were still there to provide leadership.* The work of the church at Antioch continued without Barnabas and Paul. The work was bigger than both men. It was God empowered. Bible study groups will survive just fine if talented leaders are released to serve elsewhere in the church. The work and ministry of a Bible study group is also Spirit empowered and not dependent on any one person.

If you are a group leader, keep your eyes peeled for the ones in your group who ought to be released to use their gifts and talents in the preschool, children, or student ministries of your church. Hold onto your people lightly. Loosen your grip on them. "Throw 'em back" and release them to serve.

You're Not "Just a Teacher"

A significant event happened in my life in 2019. The year before, my family discovered that my mother's physical and mental health were rapidly declining. Mom passed away on August 23, 2019. In her final week of life, she lost her balance and fell in her assisted living facility, breaking her leg. We kept her heavily sedated because she was not strong enough for surgery, according to her doctor. The Lord was gracious and called her home a few days after the accident, healing her completely. I was not present when she died around midnight on that Thursday night, but my sister Deb and my son Josh were. Even though I did not get to have the goodbye I wanted, Mom and I will have all eternity to catch up. That makes me smile. What a difference knowing Jesus makes!

In the time between Mom's death and funeral, my sister found some memorabilia that Mom had stored for safekeeping. In these boxes was a binder with typed pages that chronicled her life. She had obviously written these years ago to record the major events in her life for us. We never knew these documents existed until after her death. On one page in that binder, my mother mentioned a Sunday school teacher who taught her class when Mom was nine years old. This teacher, Helen Jensen, had no idea the impact she would have on my mother, who in turn had an impact on my sister and on me.

For the first time ever, I read the story of my mother's life in a document she wrote before her memory failed. I wept. I learned how influential Helen Jensen had been on my mother when she was in third grade. I discovered that my mother was saved at age nine. Until that moment, I never knew that Helen Jensen existed. Someone at Helen's church encouraged her to step up and serve a third-grade girls' class. I am so thankful she did. I am a life forever changed by this special lady named Helen.

I would like you to hear the influence that "just a Sunday school teacher" had on my mother. Mom wrote, *Due to the Christian influence of parents, and Sunday School teachers like Helen Jensen, I accepted Christ as my Savior in 1944. I will always have a special love for this church (University Baptist in Abilene, Texas) because that monumental decision was made there.*

The teachers who came before Ms. Jensen taught my mother about Jesus, laying a spiritual foundation. Like Scripture says, they planted, but Helen Jensen harvested. Helen Jensen was there when my mother was nine years old, right when the Holy Spirit convicted my mother of her sin and brought her to the point of repentance. Helen talked to Mom, shared the gospel, and explained how she could become a Christian. Mom accepted Christ as her Savior and was baptized a few weeks later. As Mom grew older, she learned the Bible, discovered her spiritual gifts, and served faithfully in the church for a lifetime until she had to be placed in assisted living care. Hers was a life well lived.

Helen Jensen led Mom to the Lord, and Mom made sure that my sister and I were in church (especially Sunday school) each week—no exceptions! If it snowed, we went to church. If it was raining, we went to church. I have jokingly told people I had a drug problem while growing up—Mom drug me to church every Sunday!

I surrendered to ministry, went to seminary, and went on to lead the education ministries of three churches. I currently serve as the director of Sunday School for Lifeway Christian Resources. I write, blog, teach, manage the Adult Curriculum Department whose resources are used by millions of adults weekly, and train leaders around the country. My sister has been a pastor's wife for three decades, and she and her husband have a long history of serving churches in Oklahoma and Texas. She and I are who we are today because of Christ, and we are saved because of our mother's influence as a Christian. Mom was first influenced by a West Texas Sunday school teacher who led her to Jesus at age nine.

If you lead a Bible study group, never use the phrase, "I'm just a teacher." I imagine that Helen Jensen might have thought of herself in those terms. "Just a teacher. Nobody special." She might have thought of herself as a church member doing her part because someone asked her to serve through teaching. Little did she know that she would play an important part in my mother's salvation decision and that through Mom's influence as a Christian, my sister and I would become believers and have ministries that outlived them both.

I never knew Helen Jensen existed until a few years ago, but I am thankful for her service as a Sunday school teacher. She changed my life because she taught the Bible to my mother, loved my mother, and introduced my mother to Jesus. If you lead a group, never say, *"I'm just a teacher."* You are much more than that! You are a shepherd, an evangelist, an encourager, a teacher of God's Word, and you will never know the depth and breadth of your influence on people until you get to heaven and see the results of your labor. I will guarantee you that you are making a bigger difference than you know.

> You are a shepherd, an evangelist, an encourager, a teacher of God's Word, and you will never know the depth and breadth of your influence on people until you get to heaven and see the results of your labor.

Stories like Helen Jensen's are what can happen when people are encouraged to leave groups to serve others. Are there people in Bible study groups who will become the next Helen Jensen in someone's life? The answer is a resounding yes. How could we not, as group leaders, encourage the members of our groups to step up and step out so that God can bless others through their work as volunteer leaders? The goal of Bible study groups is not to have the biggest group in the church, but to be the group that sends people out to serve.

The new scorecard for groups has a place for us to evaluate our groups by asking the question, "Are group members encouraged to serve others in the church?" How would you rate your group? Is it growing larger each year, or do you see people leaving to serve while those who remain in the group rejoice and pray for those who become leaders elsewhere in the church?

NEW SCORECARD FOR GROUPS				
		GRADE		
	ENGAGE IN ACTS OF SERVICE	A	B	C	D
13	Are groups making a difference in the community?				
14	Are group members encouraged to serve in the church?				
15					
16					

Main Ideas

1. Bible study groups should not be storehouses of people. Instead, groups should be clearinghouses from which group members are released to serve.

2. When group leaders release their best people to serve, there are always enough leaders who remain, or new ones God sends to the group, to keep the group strong and vibrant.

3. Teachers like Helen Jensen make an incredible difference in the lives of people they serve as group leaders. Every group has a Helen Jensen who needs a little encouragement to leave

the group in order to become a difference-maker in the lives of others.

Questions for Discussion

1. What is your philosophy about group members: Do you prefer to "catch and release," or do you like to "catch and keep"? What led you to have either of those mindsets with your Bible study group?

2. Which ministries in your church have a shortage of leaders? How could your group help fill some of those open positions? What is your next step?

3. Who is the Helen Jensen in your group? What person, or persons, could be encouraged to leave your group to serve other people in your church?

To-Do List

1. Ask your pastor or other staff leader about the open leadership positions in your church. Get a list and pray for each open position to be filled.

2. If your philosophy has been to "catch and keep" group members, consider the reasons for that and commit to follow the example seen in the church at Antioch in Acts 2.

3. Talk with the Helen Jensen in your group who is ready to lead a group of her own, or who is well-equipped to serve the members of your church in some other capacity. Ask the person to pray about leaving your group to become a leader elsewhere in your church.

Chapter 15

Do People Serve on the Group's Leadership Team?

I recently learned that there is a certain type of horse called a draft horse. These horses are large and muscular. They can pull large and heavy objects. The author of the article went on to describe just how much weight one horse could pull. Then he discussed the weight two horses working together could pull. I was fascinated about the implications of the story for Bible study groups. In his article, the author said the following:

> More than virtually any other animal, horses have impacted the way we humans have lived throughout most of recorded history. Many of us who have lived in the 20th and now the twenty-first centuries have no direct connection to horses, but there is still much they can teach us.
>
> Recently, I was reading about draft horses which are very large, muscular animals that, throughout history, have been used for pulling great loads and moving very

heavy objects. A single draft horse can pull a load up to 8,000 pounds. The strength involved in this is hard to imagine. So then we can speculate what would happen if we hooked up two draft horses to a load. If you instantly thought two draft horses could pull 16,000 pounds if one draft horse can pull 8,000 pounds, you would be wrong. Two draft horses pulling together cannot pull twice as much as one. They can actually pull three times as much. The two draft horses that can each pull 8,000 pounds alone can pull 24,000 pounds working together.

The horses are teaching us a very clear lesson in teamwork, but they still have more to teach us. If the two horses that are pulling together have trained with one another and have worked together before, they can't just pull three times as much working together as they can by themselves. The two trained horses in tandem can actually pull 32,000 pounds, which is a load four times as heavy as either of the horses could pull by themselves.

The powerful lessons that these magnificent draft horses can teach us involves not only teamwork but coordinated and trained collaboration. No one lives or works alone as the proverbial island unto themselves.[19]

The story of Moses and his father-in-law Jethro helps us understand how humans can work together to increase effectiveness. You may remember the story from Exodus 18. In brief, Moses sat daily to judge cases brought to him by the people. He alone served as judge. This was fine when the caseload was light, but with two million former Hebrew slaves around him, the caseload skyrocketed. The Bible reports that the people stood around Moses from dawn until dusk to have their cases heard. Most left without any legal relief.

Jethro saw what was happening and told Moses that he was not doing what was right. He advised his son-in-law to recruit and train others to share the load. Those men would judge the minor cases, and Moses would keep the more difficult ones to judge himself. In the end, working together with a group of fellow judges meant that Moses would not wear himself out, nor would he wear out and frustrate the people. The load those judges pulled together was much more than the load Moses could pull alone.

The new scorecard for groups encourages group leaders to share the load of leadership. Group leaders would be wise to remember the example of Moses and the illustration of draft horses working together to greatly increase the loads they can pull together. Group leadership can be a lot like these two scenarios. We can go about the task of teaching and leading a group by ourselves, or we can ask others to serve and pull with us. It is our choice, and it affects how much or how little we accomplish.

The Group Leadership Team

The size of a group's team will depend upon the size of the group. Smaller groups have fewer people to draw from, but the work of the group is still the same as that of larger groups. This means that smaller groups will have people who serve double duty and wear a couple of leadership hats. As the group grows, new people can be added to the team, and people who have held multiple jobs in the group can focus on only one facet of leadership. The group leadership team positions that many groups have used are:

- Teacher
- Apprentice Teacher
- Director
- Prayer Leader
- Outreach Leader
- Fellowship Leader
- Care Group Leader
- Secretary/Record Keeper
- Community Ministry Leader

Do not worry if your group is not large enough to have one person in each role; most will not be. If your group is normative, it is probably a group of ten to twelve people. In that case, people can serve in more than one role. Let's look in more detail at the job descriptions of these adult group leadership team roles.

Teacher/Group Leader

- Leads the group to study the Bible.
- Engages group members in each study through a variety of methods.
- Builds relationships with group members and guests.
- Leads group member to serve in class leadership positions.
- Leads group members to serve in the preschool, kids, or student ministries.
- Attends training events.
- Enlists an apprentice teacher for the purpose of teaching a new group.
- Leads the group to replicate and start a new one.
- Supports the pastor and staff.

Apprentice Group Leader

- Enlisted by the director.
- Teaches regularly, not just when the teacher is absent.
- Prepares to lead a group of his own.

Director

- Leads many of the administrative tasks related to group life.
- Enlists all other positions besides the teacher role (the teacher is enlisted by the pastor or his designated representative).
- Organizes the group to carry out its ministry, allowing the teacher to focus on the primary function of studying and leading effective and engaging Bible studies weekly.

Prayer Leader

- Enlisted by the director.
- Leads a time of prayer during the Bible study.
- Keeps accurate records of prayer requests.
- Informs group members of new prayer requests and updates to existing ones.
- Maintains a vibrant personal prayer life.

Outreach Leader

- Enlisted by the director.
- Responsible for keeping the group's attention on reaching new members.
- Encourages prospects and guests to enroll in the group.
- Enlists class greeters.

- Helps group members know and practice a gospel presentation.
- Helps group members develop their testimony by asking them to write their testimony and practice sharing it with the group, or in smaller groups.
- Coordinates with the information specialist to invite all prospects to class events, outings, fellowships, etc.
- Follows up with guests.
- Leads the group to wear name tags.
- Leads the group to be welcoming to guests.

Fellowship Leader

- Enlisted by the director.
- Plans a fellowship/social event at least once a quarter.
- Secures church facilities if needed.
- Includes all absentee and prospective members in communication about events, and extends invitations for them to attend.
- Includes fellow group members in the planning and implementation of fellowships/socials each quarter.
- Evaluates the response to each fellowship and the effectiveness of those events.

Care Group Leader

- Enlisted by the director.
- Responsible for shepherding a subset of the group (six to eight people).
- Prays with care group members who have requests or experience a crisis.

- Contacts the members of their care group weekly.
- Organizes the care group to meet the needs of its members; when needs exceed the group's capacity, the care group leader will seek help from other care group leaders and/or the teacher.

Greeter

- Enlisted by the outreach leader.
- Welcomes guests upon their arrival to the group's Bible study.
- Introduces guests to other members of the group.
- Coordinates with the information specialist to capture the contact information of each guest.
- Offers to sit with the guest(s) in the worship service.

Secretary/Record Keeper

- Enlisted by the director.
- Records attendance when the group meets.
- Maintains accurate guest information.
- Provides a copy of the attendance records to the teacher and care group leader.
- Notifies the teacher and care group leaders if a group member's attendance changes dramatically.
- Updates group member contact information when it changes.
- Provides the outreach leader with the contact information for all prospects.

- Assigns new group members and prospects to care group leaders.

Community Ministry Leader

- Enlisted by the director.
- Schedules four ministry/service days in the community each year.
- Leads the group's members and their families to serve others.
- Keeps a list of ways the group can serve people in the community.
- Coordinates with other groups to invite them to serve when a ministry project is too large for the group to accomplish alone.

Emerging Roles in a Digital Age

Online groups have grown significantly in recent days. That trend will likely continue, and online or hybrid groups would be wise to think in terms of adding new roles needed for a digital age. The position descriptions that follow were created by Todd Adkins and his team at Ministry Grid, an online tool created by Lifeway for training church leaders.

Digital Adult Group Director

A digital adult group director leads the implementation of biblically focused online communities. A group director serves as an administrative liaison to church staff and provides oversight of Bible study materials and group care.

- Reports to pastor or small group pastor.
- Oversees digital adult group leaders.
- Weekly time investment: five to ten hours.

Ministry Responsibilities

- Provides strategic leadership of digital adult group implementation consistent with the church's mission.
- Oversees delivery of digital adult group Bible study materials.
- Ensures ongoing group care is facilitated through digital adult group leaders.
- Recruits and trains digital adult group leaders.

Core Competencies

- Discipleship: Knows basic doctrines, practices spiritual disciplines, and exhibits the fruit of the Spirit.
- Vision: Articulates and implements vision for ministry area.
- Strategy: Leads others to unite around and execute ministry strategy.
- Collaboration: Works through others.
- People Development: Develops others.
- Stewardship: Faithfully stewards giftedness of others.

Digital Adult Group Leader

A digital adult group leader facilitates a biblically focused online community for a group. A leader monitors the spiritual growth of group members, teaches biblical truth, facilitates group discussion, and coordinates needs among group members.

- Reports to digital adult group director.
- Oversees digital adult group volunteers.
- Weekly time investment: two to five hours.

Ministry Responsibilities

- Studies weekly lesson based on Bible study materials.
- Facilitates and guides online group discussion time.
- Manages weekly online group time to ensure meeting includes prayer requests, Bible study, and discussion.
- Delegates event, outreach, and member care responsibilities to small group volunteers.
- Mentors two digital adult group volunteers with the goal of developing new leaders and starting new online communities.
- Has a working knowledge of the online meeting platform.

Core Competencies

- Discipleship: Knows basic doctrines, practices spiritual disciplines, and exhibits the fruit of the Spirit.
- Vision: Articulates and implements vision for ministry area.
- Strategy: Leads others to unite around and execute ministry strategy.
- Collaboration: Works through others.
- People Development: Develops others.
- Stewardship: Faithfully stewards giftedness of others.

Digital Adult Group Host Volunteer

The digital adult group host volunteer provides a welcoming environment to all online participants. The host volunteer sends the weekly meeting invitation to group members in advance, establishes digital meeting guidelines for the group, and controls online meeting platform permissions to provide an orderly environment for the group's online community.

- Reports to digital adult group leader.
- Weekly time investment: one to three hours.

Ministry Responsibilities

- Sends the meeting time and invitation link to the group weekly.
- Launches the online meeting early and welcomes group participants.
- Establishes digital meeting guidelines and courtesies for the group.
- Controls the permissions of the online meeting platform to ensure group time remains orderly.
- Recruits other host volunteers to assist with hosting the online community.

Core Competencies

- Discipleship: Knows the gospel and takes responsibility for personal development.
- Vision: Supports vision of ministry area.
- Strategy: Serves effectively in ministry role.
- Collaboration: Works with others.
- People Development: Displays willingness to be developed.
- Stewardship: Faithfully stewards personal giftedness.

Digital Adult Group Member Care Volunteer

The digital adult group member care volunteer organizes and facilitates care for group members. The member care volunteer is compassionate toward those who are hurting, marginalized, or celebrating during transitional times.

- Reports to digital adult group leader.
- Weekly time investment: one to three hours.

Ministry Responsibilities

- Follows up with first-time group participants.
- Reaches out to absent group members.
- Makes list of the group's prayer concerns during meeting time and sends to the group.
- Celebrates answered prayer with group members.
- Provides support and encouragement for group members in times of crisis, transition, or celebration.

Core Competencies

- Discipleship: Knows the gospel and takes responsibility for personal development.
- Vision: Supports vision of ministry area.
- Strategy: Serves effectively in ministry role.
- Collaboration: Works with others.
- People Development: Displays willingness to be developed.
- Stewardship: Faithfully stewards personal giftedness.

Digital Support Volunteer*

The digital support volunteer trains and supports digital adult group leaders and host volunteers on the online meeting platform the church uses for online communities. *Please note this role may support multiple ministries of the church.

- Reports to digital adult group director.
- Weekly time investment: three to five hours.

Ministry Responsibilities

- Trains new digital adult group leaders and hosts on how to use the online meeting platform.
- Provides information and additional training to digital adult group leaders and hosts when online meeting platform updates occur.
- Troubleshoots technical problems with online meeting platform.

Core Competencies

- Discipleship: Knows the gospel and takes responsibility for personal development.
- Vision: Supports vision of ministry area.
- Strategy: Serves effectively in ministry role.
- Collaboration: Works with others.
- People Development: Displays willingness to be developed.
- Stewardship: Faithfully stewards personal giftedness.

Digital Adult Group Porch Drop-off Coordinator*

The group porch drop-off coordinator prints, organizes, and facilitates delivery of Bible study materials to group participants. *Please note that the responsibilities of this role may be combined with those of a small group pastor or digital adult group director and may not require a separate role.

- Reports to small group pastor or digital adult group director.
- Oversees group porch drop-off volunteers.
- Weekly commitment: three to five hours.

Ministry Responsibilities

- Assembles Bible study material packets per group participant.
- Organizes packets by family.
- Groups together addresses in proximity and develops delivery zones for volunteers.
- Oversees packet pickup for volunteers.
- Oversees group porch drop-off volunteers.
- Mentors two group digital adult group volunteers with the goal of developing new group digital adult group leaders.

Core Competencies

- Discipleship: Knows basic doctrines, practices spiritual disciplines, and exhibits the fruit of the Spirit.
- Vision: Articulates and implements vision for ministry area.
- Strategy: Leads others to unite around and execute ministry strategy.
- Collaboration: Works through others.
- People Development: Develops others.
- Stewardship: Faithfully stewards giftedness of others.

Digital Adult Group Porch Drop-off Volunteer

A group porch drop-off volunteer assists with assembly and delivery of Bible study materials to group participants.

- Reports to group porch drop-off coordinator.
- Weekly commitment: one to three hours.

Ministry Responsibilities

- Picks up Bible study packets at church.
- Delivers packets to porches of group participants.
- Sends text to group participants upon delivery.
- Recruits group porch drop-off volunteers.

Core Competencies

- Discipleship: Knows the gospel and takes responsibility for personal development.
- Vision: Supports vision of ministry area.
- Strategy: Serves effectively in ministry role.
- Collaboration: Works with others.
- People Development: Displays willingness to be developed.
- Stewardship: Faithfully stewards personal giftedness.

Shared leadership is good leadership.

We are better together, and we are better when we are serving together, pulling in the same direction. One of the new scorecard measurements for groups is how well group members take ownership for the group and fill leadership roles.

Shared leadership is good leadership. And in the end, the group will be more effective as people use their God-given spiritual gifts to serve their fellow group members.

Do the people in your group pull together and serve others in the group as members of a group leadership team? Evaluate your group below.

NEW SCORECARD FOR GROUPS					
			GRADE		
	ENGAGE IN ACTS OF SERVICE	A	B	C	D
13	Are groups making a difference in the community?				
14	Are group members encouraged to serve in the church?				
15	Do people serve on the group's leadership team?				
16					

Main Ideas

1. Savvy group leaders delegate the work of the group to others who help accomplish important tasks. Unless the workload is divided, many group leaders will experience burnout as they attempt to do everything themselves.

2. Group members are spiritually gifted and can serve alongside their group leader to accomplish the work of ministry.

3. Group members can serve in an on-campus group in numerous ways, and with the advent of online groups, new leadership opportunities abound.

Questions for Discussion

1. What keeps group leaders from delegating more of the work of their groups? How might group leaders benefit by enlisting others to help carry the load?

2. Why are group members not asked to serve on their group's leadership team? If group members did serve, how would this change the dynamics of groups?

3. If group members are not asked to serve, what is the end result?

To-Do List

1. Use the lists of possible group leadership positions in this chapter to create your own list of leadership roles needed in your Bible study group. Combine positions if necessary.

2. Identify one group leader for each open position on your new list of needed leadership roles. Begin praying that each person with whom you speak will respond favorably to serving the members of the group in that role.

3. Set a date to talk with your Bible study group members about the need to involve them in the work of your group. Explain the leadership roles and their basic tasks. Invite group members to pray about serving in a leadership capacity.

Chapter 16

Does the Group Encourage and Pray for the Pastor?

Pastoring is hard work.

I have been in ministry since my calling in 1988. Some classmates with whom I attended seminary are no longer in the ministry. Some gave in to temptations and disqualified themselves from further ministry. Those situations were terrible to observe. Some of those leaders recovered after a season of repentance and healing and are once again serving a congregation. Others did not make it, and marriages and ministries ended.

The pandemic that started in 2020 brought increased pressures on pastors and staff. Congregational situations changed dramatically from week to week. Worship services moved online in less than two weeks at the beginning of the outbreak, as did financial giving—two things that most churches were not accustomed to doing. Pastors took criticism from church members who felt their churches were operating in fear; others felt the church was not taking any precautions. People often responded to their pastors based on political affiliations. Hard work got harder.

And in the meantime, the work of ministry went on as pastors had to figure out how to juggle a whole new set of issues and expectations brought about by the pandemic.

Lifeway Research published an article about pastors and the difficulties they face daily. The article shed light on a side of pastoring that most of us do not think about. We typically see our pastors as preachers in the pulpit. The article from Lifeway, however, revealed the following about the typical workweek of a pastor:

> Consider for a moment the fact that almost every task a pastor has is by nature complex: studying for a sermon, giving marital advice, providing leadership to a volunteer organization, having budget responsibility, helping those who are grieving, etc. That diverse complexity alone is taxing.
>
> But the demands on a pastor require them to quickly switch between different complex tasks that require completely different knowledge, skills, or abilities. Matt Bloom is Associate Professor at the University of Notre Dame where he leads the Wellbeing at Work Program. He describes the toll that this takes on a pastor. The switching, "is costly in terms of cognitive effort, behavioral control, and emotion regulation."
>
> And this list of tasks for a pastor never ends. There is always another complex task to switch to and to pour your all into.
>
> A congregation's needs, demands, and desires seem never-ending and are often ill-timed.[20]

Some of you reading this book may not have a full-time pastor. The person who leads your congregation is bi-vocational, works a full-time job during the week, and serves your congregation on Sunday, Wednesday, and other times as he is available. The bi-vocational pastor has a unique set of pressures on him. Not only does he have the responsibility to feed and care for his family through his full-time job, but he also has a congregation that expects him to preach, teach, serve, and relate to them. I know a few bi-vocational pastors, and their work can be exhausting. The truth is that a significant number of churches are led by bi-vocational pastors. Still more are led by a single staff person—the pastor—and everything falls on him. If you happen to be one of these kinds of pastors, God bless you! Thank you for serving the Lord the way you do.

On the other end of the church spectrum are congregations that number in the thousands, maybe even the tens of thousands. These megachurches have pastors who face entirely different sets of challenges and pressures that normative size churches do not. Ministry is complex in these churches. Hundreds upon hundreds of volunteer workers are needed to staff ministries each week. Recruitment never ends. The staff organizational chart is complex. The congregation expects and demands excellence. It is a high-pressure environment indeed.

My brother-in-law, Dr. Ron Brown, is a pastor of a church in Cleburn, Texas. While in seminary, he pastored a small church in southern Oklahoma. That church had one of those "number" boards at the front of the worship center. You might know the kind I am talking about. It kept a record of last Sunday's attendance and giving and year-to-date giving. On most Sundays, the news it contained was not great, and Ron noticed that people would come into the worship center, look at the sign board, and then hang their heads. One

Sunday he announced that he planned to remove the board and hang it somewhere else because it was interfering with the people's worship. The next morning, though, he got a phone call from the matriarch of the church who told him, and I quote, "Pastor, if you remove that board, you can start packing up your office."

I've had experiences similar to the ones my brother-in-law had. I recently served a small church as a part-time discipleship pastor and was called a liar for reporting what one person in my church thought were elevated attendance numbers. Others accused me of having an agenda because I advocated the purchase or lease of portable buildings so the congregation could continue to start new adult Sunday school groups. My detractors said I was bent on turning the church's property into a "mobile home park." One adult teacher, a deacon whose class my wife and I visited for several weeks when we first joined the church's staff, confronted me after class one Sunday. Tammy and I were going to join his group because he was a good, well-prepared teacher. After our third or fourth visit to his group, he declared his suspicions about us after class one Sunday by saying to us, "I don't appreciate you coming into my group to spy on me!" He said those words while unsuccessfully restraining his anger. My wife and I were simply looking for a group to join.

At that same church, a member of a women's class confronted me when I would not allow her teacher to create her own Bible studies. I explained to her that I ask all group leaders to follow a curriculum plan. She told me that "this was her church long before I took it over." Her complaints led the personnel team to uninvite me to be a part of the staff. (Did I mention that she was a member of the personnel team?) All of that took place after I practiced Romans 12:14–21 with her and offered to meet with her, pray for her, and try to help her move past her anger. I told her that I forgave her, which caused her to unleash a flurry of angry words at me. It was to no avail; her immaturity and selfishness would not allow for any reconciliation. I could go on, but suffice it to say, *pastoring is hard work.*

Lift High Your Pastor's Hands

Pastors today are in a difficult position. It seems any decision they make pleases half their congregation and causes the other half to shake their heads, murmur, withdraw, or leave. I am sure you will remember the story of Moses in Exodus 17. The Israelites had engaged the Amalekites in battle. Here is the description of what happened:

> While Moses held up his hand, Israel pre-
> vailed, but whenever he put his hand down,
> Amalek prevailed. When Moses's hands
> grew heavy, they took a stone and put it
> under him, and he sat down on it. Then
> Aaron and Hur supported his hands, one
> on one side and one on the other so that his
> hands remained steady until the sun went
> down. So Joshua defeated Amalek and his
> army with the sword. (vv. 11–13)

Leaders like Moses have limited strength. Moses realized he needed people around him who would stand with him and help Israel gain victory over the Amalekites. That is when Aaron and Hur entered the picture. They held up Moses's hands and Israel won.

Your pastor needs you. He is most likely physically and spiritually tired. Groups must commit to encourage pastors, not nip at their heels. We must be gracious and forgiving to our leaders. We should choose to believe that they are hearing from God and leading the congregation in a direction ordained by Him. Stand with your pastor. Encourage him. Pray for his family and ministry. Follow his leadership, and love him as Christ loves you.

If you have a genuine concern about the church in which you are a member, do not gossip. Do not share your concerns as a prayer request in the Bible study group. Instead, meet with your pastor privately and hear him out. Share your perspective. Ask questions respectfully, not with an accusatory tone. Compromise on the nonessentials. Do not rally the troops against the pastor, but instead, pray for him and vigorously attempt to see things from his point of view. Accept his decisions. Follow his leadership. Be kind.

Lift high the hands of your pastor.

Praying as Serving

One of the greatest ways any Bible study group can serve is to pray. James 5:16 reminds us that the prayers of God's people are powerful and effective. While many of the prayers in our groups focus on the needs of group members, their families, friends, and coworkers, we must not forget to pray for our pastor. If your church is large enough to have multiple staff leaders, remember to pray for them as well.

The senior saints among us at church are wonderful because so many of them have learned that having a ministry of prayer is as important as having any other job in the church, maybe even more important. If I ever needed prayer for something in my life, I knew to go to the groups with our oldest members because they always took the privilege of prayer seriously. Other Bible study groups can learn this, too. Groups with median and young adults can have a significant ministry of prayer for the pastor and staff.

Twelve Things to Pray for Your Pastor Every Year

As you lead your group to pray for your pastor and staff leaders, there are several ways to pray for them. You may choose to pray for only one of these at a time (perhaps selecting one each month), or your group might choose to have a night of prayer, praying through the entire list in one extended prayer time. Whatever you decide, the important thing is that you focus attention on your pastor and staff through prayer.

1. Pray that your pastor would guard his doctrine closely.
2. Pray for your pastor's family.
3. Pray for a hedge of protection around your pastor.
4. Pray your pastor hears and discerns God's voice through prayer and Bible reading.
5. Pray for your pastor's health and mental well-being.
6. Pray for your pastor to have great wisdom to lead the church well.
7. Pray your pastor continues to grow in the fruit of the Spirit.
8. Pray for your pastor to be encouraged about the church and his ministry.
9. Pray for your pastor to bear up well when criticized and to forgive those who harm him.
10. Pray for your pastor to rest in God's financial provision.
11. Pray for your pastor to live a faithful life of service.
12. Pray for God to use your pastor in ways that increase his influence for the kingdom.

Oxygen to the Soul

I once heard it said that praise is like oxygen to a person's soul. I like that. It is true: we all need encouragement and a slap on the back from time to time. It's nice to know that others see our good work, our good character, and our attempts to serve the Lord with all our heart, mind, soul, and strength.

Groups can play a part in supporting the pastor by intentionally and authentically taking time to praise him for his good work. Group leaders should remind group members to regularly thank the pastor for any ministry he does directly to and for them. Having a box of thank-you cards available for group members to quickly write a note of encouragement is just one way groups can lift up their pastor. A group could collect money to purchase a gift card for the pastor—perhaps one to his favorite restaurant, sporting goods store, or Christian bookstore. A group could help him by cutting his grass one week to give him a Saturday back for a family outing. A group could provide a series of meals one week to relieve him and his wife of the daily drudgery of selecting which meals to prepare for their family; instead, let him know that each night at 5:00 p.m., a member of your group will bring his family a meal. Things like this put a spring in the step of our pastors, and it takes just a little effort to do so much for our pastors and their families.

The idea here is to make this a part of the natural rhythm of your group's life. Be known for being your pastor's biggest supporter. Be the group he talks about to his pastor friends!

We have almost reached the end of our journey together. We have discovered there are more ways to evaluate the success and effectiveness of Bible study groups besides recording attendance. In this final evaluation, how would you rate your group when it comes to praying for and supporting your pastor? The other members of the church's leadership team? Do that now, then respond to the questions that follow.

NEW SCORECARD FOR GROUPS				
		GRADE		
ENGAGE IN ACTS OF SERVICE	A	B	C	D
13	Are groups making a difference in the community?			
14	Are group members encouraged to serve in the church?			
15	Do people serve on the group's leadership team?			
16	**Does the group encourage and pray for the pastor?**			

Main Ideas

1. Pastoring is hard work, and our church's leaders need prayer, support, and encouragement from us.

2. Groups can work together to provide support for pastors through encouraging notes, gifts, acts of kindness, and ongoing prayers.

3. Pastors experience challenges, setbacks, and discouragement. Both they and their families need to be blessed and encouraged to remain faithful to the Lord despite the difficulties of ministry.

Questions for Discussion

1. Does your church have a history of discouraging or encouraging pastors? What kind of tenures do the pastors at your church have?

2. What are some immediate, practical ways your Bible study group can become a source of encouragement to your pastor and to all the members of your church staff?

3. Is there a person or a group of people in your church who have a history of unnecessarily confronting the pastor or staff? With whom can you talk about this pattern so that biblical confrontation can take place to end the destructive pattern?

To-Do List

1. If you have been the source of antagonism toward your pastor, repent of those actions, seek his forgiveness, and become an advocate for him.

2. Choose to speak words of blessing over your pastor; resist the temptation to talk derisively about him.

3. Lay the groundwork with your Bible study group to set a new precedent for speaking in positive, uplifting ways about your pastor. Lead them to honor and support his ministry and his family.

Epilogue

I began this book with the words, "I love golf." Even more important, I love the church and love what takes place through a church's Bible teaching ministry. It has been my ministry calling for years to help churches reach people, disciple people, and release people to serve in a variety of ways.

This book combined those two of my passions. Through the illustration of a golf scorecard, I communicated the need for churches to take a different look at how we measure the success of Bible study groups. For so long, the church has evaluated the effectiveness of groups by measuring attendance only.

The new scorecard for groups has served to focus on four measurements of group life. Attendance is still a metric we'll want to measure, but think about what might take place in your group, or in the groups at your church, if all of them accomplished these four goals:

- Learn and obey God's Word.
- Invite people to become disciples.
- Form deeper relationships.
- Engage in acts of service.

To help evaluate groups, I asked sixteen questions, four related to each of the new scorecard measurements above.

Taken together, these four measurements and sixteen questions give us a way to discover our strengths and weaknesses so that we can work to improve them. In golf, this is the way I have improved my game over the years. I've measured key aspects of my game and worked on improving the ones that were not up to par (no pun intended).

At the end of each chapter, I asked you to evaluate your Bible study group based on one of the sixteen questions. You rated your group on a grading scale: A-B-C-D. *Now I would like you to use the new group scorecard on the following pages and transfer your responses to it.* This will give you a singular way to view your group. It will also help identify those areas in which you and your group need to improve.

My encouragement for you is to focus on any of the sixteen questions that you graded as a C or a D. Start with those, make improvements, and then move on to improve the ones you rated as a B. This is going to take time, so do not be hard on yourself or your group! As in the game of golf, improvements take time.

May God bless you and your group as you continually make disciples in obedience to His command.

THE NEW SCORECARD FOR GROUPS				
	GRADE			
MEASUREMENT 1: LEARN AND OBEY GOD'S WORD	A	B	C	D
1 Are group members growing as disciples?				
2 Are Bible studies well prepared and engaging?				
3 Are apprentice leaders identified and developed?				
4 Are new groups started regularly?				
MEASUREMENT 2: INVITE PEOPLE TO BECOME DISCIPLES	A	B	C	D
5 Are prayers focused on the lost?				
6 Are group members eating with "sinners and tax collectors"?				
7 Are new persons invited to connect with the group?				
8 Are group members initiating gospel conversations?				
MEASUREMENT 3: FORM DEEPER RELATIONSHIPS	A	B	C	D
9 Are groups organized to care for people?				
10 How balanced are connection and content?				
11 Do newcomers experience biblical hospitality?				
12 Are microgroups strengthening relationships?				
MEASUREMENT 4: ENGAGE IN ACTS OF SERVICE	A	B	C	D
13 Are groups making a difference in the community?				

14	Are group members encouraged to serve in the church?				
15	Do people serve on the group's leadership team?				
16	Does the group encourage and pray for the pastor?				

About the Author

Ken Braddy is the director of Sunday School at Lifeway Christian Resources. He trains pastors, group leaders, and others in the best practices of groups. Ken also manages the team at Lifeway that produces ongoing Bible studies used by approximately three million adults every week. He led the Sunday school of his first church to grow from forty-four members to more than twenty-four hundred members. He led a Nashville area church to become the fastest growing Sunday school in Tennessee by percentage growth.

Ken has a large following at his groups blog (kenbraddy.com), and he has coauthored or authored seven books on group ministry in the local church. He has authored or compiled seven books on Sunday school and small groups and has written numerous articles for *Facts & Trends Magazine,* Outreach.com, ChurchLeader.com, and Lifeway Voices. His six-session Bible study in the Bible Studies for Life series was studied by 1.6 million adults and teens.

Ken is a frequent guest on the *Group Answers* podcast, and he speaks and trains at events around the country. He and his wife, Tammy, have started two Bible study groups recently. They have two grown children and two grandchildren.

Notes

1. Philip Nation, "Recognizing Transformation," Bible Studies for Life.

2. "Apprenticeship," *Britannica*, accessed December 20, 2021, https://www.britannica.com/topic/apprenticeship.

3. John Maxwell, *Developing the Leaders Around You: How to Help Others Reach Their Full Potential* (Nashville: Thomas Nelson, 1995), 99–101.

4. "Grand Canyon National Park Trips," *Outside*, November 5, 2019, https://www.mygrandcanyonpark.com/park/faqs/falling-to-death-grand-canyon.

5. Steve Parr, *Sunday School That Really Works: A Strategy for Connecting Congregations and Communities* (Grand Rapids, MI: Kregel Academic & Professional: 2010), 63.

6. David Francis, *Connect3* (Nashville: Lifeway Press, 2008), 19.

7. Scott McConnell, *Together: The Power of Groups* (Nashville: Lifeway Press, 2020) 16.

8. Roger Schiffman, "How to Practice like a Pro," *Golf Digest*, March 8, 2011, https://www.golfdigest.com/story/how-to-practice-like-a-pro#:~:text=In%20a%20day%2C%20the%20average,balls%20or%20blindly%20rolling%20putts.

9. David Francis and Ken Braddy, *Three Roles for Guiding Groups* (Nashville: Lifeway Press, 2013), 8.

10. Ken Hemphill, *Revitalizing the Sunday Morning Dinosaur: A Sunday School Growth Strategy for the 21st Century* (Nashville: B&H, 1996), 123.

11. Carey Nieuwhof, "8 Disruptive Church Trends That Will Rule 2021 (the Rise of the Post-pandemic Church), Carey Nieuwhof, https://careynieuwhof.com/8-disruptive-church-trends-that-will-rule-2021-the-rise-of-the-post-pandemic-church.

12. McConnell, *Together: The Power of Groups*, 12.

13. Ryan Dabbs, "Social Media Reacts to Improved Charles Barkley Golf Swing," *Golf Monthly*, May 6, 2021, https://www.golfmonthly.com/news/social-media-reacts-to-charles-barkley-improved-golf-swing-231358.

14. Ken Hemphill, *Ten Best Practices: To Make Your Sunday School Work* (Nashville: Lifeway Press, 2001), 155.

15. McConnell, *Together: The Power of Groups*, 24.

16. Ibid., 19.

17. David Francis, *Great Expectations: Planting Seeds for Sunday School Growth* (Nashville: Lifeway Press, 2010), 29.

18. Jeff Irog, *The Case for Antioch: A Biblical Model for Transformational Church* (Nashville: B&H Publishing Group, 2011).

19. Jim Stoval, "Horse Sense," Tim Maurer, https://tim-maurer.com/2012/01/16/horse-sense.

20. Scott McConnell, "Are More Pastors Quitting Today?," Lifeway Research, May 13, 2021, https://lifewayresearch.com/2021/05/13/are-more-pastors-quitting-today.